Babylon

Babylon

Dipak K. Das

ISPCK
Impacting Communities since 1710

Tercentenary Publication
2010

Babylon - Published by Rev. Dr. Ashish Amos of the Indian Society for Promoting Christian Knowledge (ISPCK), Post Box 1585, 1654, Madarsa Road, Kashmere Gate, Delhi-110006.

ISBN: 978-81-8465-103-4

Laser typeset by

ISPCK, Post Box 1585, 1654, Madarsa Road, Kashmere Gate, Delhi-110006 • *Tel:* 23866323

e-mail: ashish@ispck.org.in • ella@ispck.org.in
website: www.ispck.org.in

Dedicated to my Parents
late Jogesh Chandra Das and
late Sushila Das

Contents

Preface

I would like to express my thanks to my wife, Ratna, and my daughters, Sonali and Kakoli, for their co-operation, without which I could not have finished this book.

I would also like to express my thanks retrospectively to my father, late Jogesh Chandra Das, who was a life-long evangelist in Silchar Presbyterian Church (Assam, India) and my mother, late Sushila Das, who also served the Lord according to her capacity.

I take this opportunity to thank all those who indirectly helped me in bringing out this book.

Last, but not the least, I would like to thank the ISPCK General Secretary Rev. Dr. Ashish Amos for agreeing to publish this book.

July 2009.

Dr. D. K. Das.

Kolkata, West Bengal

Introduction

God is the author of the Universe. Every human being is predestined (Isa. 46:10; Dan 4:35; Acts 4:28; Rom. 8:29,30; Ephy. 1:11), for God sees beforehand and 'predestines' what will happen. He predestines the Universe; the Universe obeys His rule. He predestines nations; for example, the Israelites (Isa. 65:9, 22). He predestines individuals; for example, Moses, Abraham, Jacob, David and Jesus. Because God is the ruler of the Universe, there is nothing wrong in what He does. He is perfect in power and wisdom, and all the things he has created move in accordance with His will (Ps. 33: 10, 11; Prov. 16: 33; Isa. 14: 26, 27; 37: 26, 27; Acts 17:26, 27; Rom. 8:29, 30; Eph. 1:5, 6:1 Pet. 1:20). It was God who wanted Jesus Christ (Isa. 42: 1) to come to the world as a Saviour.

Likewise Jesus could foresee that his disciple Peter would deny Him thrice. Again, he rode on a donkey in fulfilment of a prophecy. He also foreknew about His death (Matt. 16: 21-26; 17:22, 23; 20:17-19; Mk 8:31-33; 10:32-34; Lk. 9: 22- 27; 9: 44; 18: 31- 34). Jesus said, "not my will, but thine, be done" (Lk. 22:42). Jesus also foretold his resurrection (Matt. 16:21; Mk. 8: 31; 10:34; Lk. 9:22). In other words, Jesus did not do anything on His own.

Jesus' second coming has also been predicted. About his second coming he said, "for as the lightning come out of the east, and shineth even unto the west; so shall also the coming of the Son of man be" (Matt. 24: 30; Mk, 13: 26; Lk 21: 27; Rev. 22:12).

Whatever the prophets foretold is coming true. Prophets are interpreters of the Divine will. They are messengers and sovereign ambassadors of God. Prophets are usually led by the Holy Spirit; they fall into a trance and foretell the future course of events. It is somewhat like a dream or a vision, with explanations in symbolic languages, or it may be like a poem. Nobody can predict what will happen except the prophets (2 Pet1: 20, 21).

Prophecies can be of two types: the short period and the long period. Jesus' prophesy before his so-called final judgement about Peter's denial of him can be considered as a short-period prophecy.

As far as long-period prophecy is concerned, prophets like Jeremiah, Isaiah, Joshua, Ezekiel, Zephaniah, Daniel and John (the disciple of Christ) had been writing about Israel, Egypt, Babylon, and Jerusalem mostly in a symbolic language.

This book contains the predictions made by a host of prophets about the destiny of Babylon.

CHAPTER I

Tale of Adam

It was many years ago when God created the universe. He created all living beings including man—His best creation. His name was Adam. But Adam turned out to be a rival to God when he fell into sin. He committed the 'original sin' and brought judgement upon himself and the whole human race. Without him death could not have been universal in character and the doctrine of the original sin would not have existed. Adam's disobedience took all living beings and the earth into the realms of pain, suffering and death. His blunder, so to say, deeply affected all mankind. He predisposed all his descendants to evil. This is why all of us have a tendency to commit sin.

Romans 3:23 says, "For all have sinned, and come short of the glory of God." What is this awful sin that attracts eternal condemnation unless we get saved by Jesus? Why should mankind continue to suffer the nemesis of Adam's mistake? What does the phrase 'they disobeyed God' mean? Lord God forbade Adam from eating of the tree of the knowledge of good and evil, "for in the day that thou eatest thereof thou shalt surely die" (Gen. 2:17). That was the first commandment of God to mankind. It had the ingredients of all spiritual laws that God wanted humans to live up to.

It appears that sin existed even before God gave the first commandment. This is quite evident in Adam's tale. Before getting trapped by Satan, Adam was like an angel. But sin, though suppressed, was inherent in him. God knew that Adam was highly susceptible to temptation, hence the need for the first commandment.

Bible experts have interpreted the tale of Adam in different ways, but only some of them have allowed it to speak for itself. Most of them have tried to read interpretations into it rather than derive interpretations from it. The divine perspective of the first two chapters of the book of Genesis, in most cases, has been overshadowed by the commentator's perspective, which has vitiated the superb artistic design of the tale. To understand the true significance of this tale, it is necessary to view the sequence of events from the divine perspective.

Also, it is worth noting that although the story of man's creation starts from Genesis 2:7, the name Adam does not figure till the eighteenth verse of the second chapter. Only the collective noun 'man' is used. Secondly, most writers overlook the fact that God gave the first commandment to Adam alone. Eve did not exist when God forbade Adam from eating of the tree of the knowledge of good and evil. In that case, Eve should not be blamed for playing a seductive role in the story. It seems Eve was informed about it later.

Likewise, when God expelled Adam from the Garden, He expelled Adam alone. He cursed Eve for playing a seductive role. The Bible says, "Therefore the Lord God sent him forth from the Garden of Eden..." (Gen. 3:23) and "So he drove out the man..." (Gen 3:24). Interestingly, Adam is blamed throughout the Bible for disobeying God, especially in the New Testament. Eve has always evaded the opprobrium (except 1 Tim. 2:14). It was Eve who was tempted by the serpent, and it was she who yielded to enticement and allured Adam to eat the forbidden fruit. If the scripture is to do any justice, it should blame Eve first, which has not been fully done. The scripture makes Adam the scapegoat. Should we conclude that there is something intrinsically wrong with the scripture? Many readers fail to understand the true significance of the tale of Adam mainly because they interpret it incorrectly. We must not regard this tale as a fairy tale, as it is replete with many shades of meaning.

Consider, for example, the name 'Adam.' Strange as it may seem, it has been used as a collective noun. The Hebrew word *Adam* also means *mankind*. There was also something known as *Adamic* civilisation. Some critics may say that Adam has been referred to by Jesus, apostle Paul and others as 'one man' and that *his* sin embraces the entire mankind. It may be because they did not at that time deem it fit to elaborate on it. The divine will unfolds truths and mysteries in a progressive manner. For example, Jesus confessed that He did not know about the second coming; only God the Father knew about it (Matt. 24:36). It is believed that since Jesus was in His human form He was not omniscient like God. But a constituent part of 'Triune God' is scarcely supposed to have been robbed of this prophetic faculty. It seems that at that point of time God chose not to disclose it. The representative name *Adam* envelopes mankind as a whole, not just Eve. The will of God is sometimes so difficult to discern.

Let us reconsider the creation of Eve. The removal of Adam's rib and the emergence of Eve are not a structural necessity of the story but a delicate way of splitting a man's mind into two of its constituent parts. The human mind has two faces. Both Jekyll and Hyde exist in each individual. Duplex is the human mind and so is the method by which it has been framed. The bifurcation of the seemingly one mind of man necessitated the adoption of the unique method of representing the same mind as two individuals. The revelation has its biblical back-up. It is written in the Bible "And Adam said, this is now bone of my bones and flesh of my flesh..." (Gen. 2:23). It implies in a tactful way that Eve was not another individual; she was in Adam. But she had a different mental disposition (often antagonistic to Adam), as though, he was a different person. Gen. 2:24 reads: "... and shall cleave unto his wife and they shall be one flesh." The emphasis here is on "one flesh", which also implies that Eve is not another entity; she had existed in Adam, in the same body. There is an Adam and Eve in every mind. Adam is spiritually inclined, not attached to worldly attractions, upright and sincere, while Eve is worldly-minded, prone to yield to lust and temptation. The human mind is like Janus, the ancient Italian two-faced God. It is also analogous to the Moon, having a bright side (the pious mind) and its dark counterpart (the impious mind).

The original men were simple in every way, and God appreciated the life they lived. According to the book of Genesis, God used to visit them and talk to them. This shows that God approved of their way of life.

The dismal part of this story starts from the point where security, comfort, luxury, convenience, material prosperity and power become their main concerns. The weaker part of the human mind (Eve) yields to temptation and prevails upon its nobler counterpart. This is why Paul encourages us by saying "Be not overcome of evil, but overcome evil with good." (Rom. 12:21). It implies that we should subjugate the impious part of our mind by the pious part. The serpent in the story is only a symbol of the temptation that our impious part of mind is always susceptible to. The serpent, the ugly-looking monster, who always fights with God by misleading God's people, is not an extraneous entity, an adversary of God loitering between heaven and earth (Job 1:6 – 12), but a symbol of temptation. So mysterious is the polarisation of mind.

The Garden of Eden as described in the Bible appears to be a beautiful park. Indeed, our mother earth is such a beautiful garden. It can neither be truly represented in its varied form by a single artificial park or garden nor be made by humans without copying the ideas from the enormous vast garden where we have to live in. Our imagination cannot surpass the knowledge of this world. One German philosopher is known to have remarked that if one dislikes the world, one may try to create another world of one's own choice; but without incorporating any ideas of this unworthy world is just impossible. Our perception of anything does not transcend our knowledge of this world. The Garden of Eden is thus not an unearthly, celestial place; it is this beautiful, green planet of ours, which has very aptly been called a *garden*.

In the book of Genesis, trees appear to symbolise God's good gifts. An interesting thing about the tree of the knowledge of good and evil is that unless we eat its fruit, we will have no inclination to stretch our hand towards the other tree, the fruit of which promises us eternal life, if eaten. In other words, the fruit of the tree of the knowledge of good and evil is only a stepping stone towards the tree of life. This is why no attempt was made to guard the tree of life before man ate of the tree of the knowledge of good and evil.

The author of the epistle to the Hebrews says, "Of whom we have many things to say, and hard to be uttered, seeing we are dull of hearing. For when for the time ye ought to be teachers, ye have need that one teach you again which be the first principle of the oracles of God, and are become such as have need of milk, and not of strong meat. For every one that useth milk is unskilful in the word of righteousness; for he is a babe. But strong meat belongeth to them that are of full age, even those who by reason of use have their senses exercised to discern both good and evil" (Heb. 5:11–14). That situation prevails even today. But the question that has haunted the minds of many a serious thinker for thousands of years is, what is the tree of the knowledge of good and evil? We ought to realise that the tree and the things associated with it in the tale of Adam are only symbolic representations. A clear evidence of this fact is the use of human language by a snake. It stands to reason that the tree is not a real tree, the fruit is not a real fruit and the snake is not a real snake. They are allegorical things.

The purpose of religion, scriptures, moral education, catechism, ethics, the Ten Commandments and so on is to impart the knowledge of good and evil, to distinguish between good and evil and to declare that we ought to hold fast to everything that is good and eschew all that is evil. Amos, the prophet, gives counsel saying, "Hate the evil and love the good (Amos 5:15). David brings the allegation that "Thou lovest evil more than good; and lying rather than speak righteousness" (Ps. 52:3). Again, Paul suggests "Let love be without dissimulation. Abhor that which is evil: cleave to that which is good "(Rom. 12:9). Also, God accuses the leaders of the Israelites saying "And I said, Hear, I pray you, O heads of Jacob, and ye princess of the house of Israel; Is it not for you to know judgement? Who hate the good, and love the evil; who pluck off their skin from off them, and their flesh from off their bones" (Micah 3:1,2).

God prohibited Adam from knowing about the nature of good and evil. We are told at the same time that only God knew about the true nature of good and evil but He did not consider it to be expedient on the part of man to know about it. When Adam and Eve ate the forbidden fruit, God exclaimed "...Behold, the man is become as one of us, to know good and evil: "(Gen 3:22). It leads to the understanding that the knowledge of good and evil represents a particular quality of God, which, He feels is detrimental to human welfare. Many readers fail to grasp the true meaning of the tale of Adam because they do not understand the figurative language in the Holy Scripture.

The body of knowledge that can be regarded as both "good" and "evil" is "science." Science had contributed enormously to human welfare. Modern people just cannot live without the aid of science and technology. Our transport system, medicine, communication network and so on are all gifts of science and technology. But has it not become a Frankenstein as well? Is it not because of the unthinkable progress of science and technology that modern civilisation is inching towards total catastrophe? Our planet will be destroyed not by intelligent beings from some other planet, but by us.

It is advisable to know the meanings of some of the words used in the Bible. The fruit of the tree of the knowledge of good and evil was looked upon as *food*. In Sanskrit, *food* stands for not only the things we eat and drink but whatever enters us. It may be an idea or a principle. Interestingly, Jesus used the word *food* in the same sense. For example, Jesus said "My *food* is to obey the will of the one who sent me and to finish the work he gave me to do. "(Jn. 4:34 TEV). It is clear that He is referring to two things within Himself, namely obedience to the Father and fulfilment of his 'mission.' He called these His *food*. Here *food* implies a particular activity as well. Adam was prohibited from getting involved in an activity that could enable him to learn about science and technology. But he ate the fruit. In other words, he engaged himself in the acquisition of scientific knowledge, only to destroy himself (mankind).

In the Holy Scripture, we see God warning: "…Of every tree of the garden thou mayest freely eat; But of the tree of the knowledge of good and evil, thou shall not eat of it; for the day that thou eatest thereof thou shall surely die." (Gen. 2: 16, 17).

The verse can be paraphrased as "you may engage yourself in all other activities but do not acquire scientific knowledge lest it should become a Frankenstein and destroy you." Indeed God had the foreknowledge about man manufacturing nuclear warheads, laser-beams, and so on, to devastate the world.

However, the advancement of science and technology continued unabated because it made our lives more secure and comfortable. The 'scientific' knowledge opened man's eyes and enabled him to become almost as powerful as God (*Behold, the man is become like one of us, to know good and evil*). The quest for ephemeral pleasure drove Adam to opt for 'science.'

The creative faculty in man is akin to the creative power of God. "The greatest gift of God to mankind is undoubtedly a marvellous brain which is the most complex aggregation of matter in the universe and a unique attribute of the image of God. "(The Remarkable Record of Job, p 106). Man did not create the brain, God crated it, as pointed out by Job: "But where shall wisdom be found? And where is the place of understanding? (Job 28:12). Also, "who hath put wisdom in the inward parts? Or who hath given understanding to the heart?" (Job 38:36).

In the book of Genesis, the use of the expression "good and evil" instead of the word 'science' is of great significance. "Good and evil" is a well thought-out expression. Its meaning does not change with changing times, though languages undergo big changes. A word or term can become obsolete but its definition or the idea it embodies remains unchanged.

The expression "good and evil" embodies the idea of 'science and technology.' The Bible was written not just for the people of ancient times. It was written for modern man as well.

Adam was banished from the Garden of Eden because he had eaten of the tree of the knowledge of good and evil. To put it in the words we use today, it was his acquisition of 'scientific knowledge' that attracted God's wrath and led to his expulsion from the Garden.

Knowledge is power. By acquiring the knowledge of good and evil, or scientific knowledge, man tried to become as powerful as God — an act that spelled doom for him. Knowledge instils false pride in man and makes him arrogant, and God hates haughtiness and vanity. He humbles the eyes of arrogant people and rewards the humble and the meek.

The period beginning the first appearance of humans on earth and ending man's fall may be called the first "Adam Cycle." This cycle can be attributed to man's pride in the progress he had made or his acquisition of scientific knowledge. "Pride goeth before destruction, and a haughty spirit before a fall" (Prov. 16:18). It is written in Psalms:

When he maketh inquisition for
blood, he remembereth them,
he forgetteth not the cry of the
humble.

(Ps. 9:12)

Again the Psalmist sings:

The meek will he guide in judgement:
And the meek will he teach his way.

(Ps. 25:9)

To pin-point what exactly happened after destruction, the Psalmist says:

> The Lord lifteth up the meek:
> He casteth the wicked down to the ground.

> (Ps. 147:6)

God abhors the 'scientific adventure' of men but rescues the humble (or the innocent people). James says:

> ...God resisteth the proud,
> But giveth grace to the humble

> (James 4:6)

Lord's servants have declared that abstinence from the dangerous 'game of science' would preclude unnecessary loss of human life and that humans would continue to thrive in this world. Consider, for instance, the following verses:

> Humble yourself in the sight of the Lord, and he shall lift you up.

> (James 4:10)

> Humble yourself therefore under the mighty hand of God, that he may exalt you in due time.

> (1 Pet 5: 6)

Are innocent children free of the original sin? Jesus blessed children and remarked that the kingdom of heaven is for them. But the word 'all' in Romans 3:23 is all inclusive. It includes children. We are faced with two apparently contradictory statements here. This contradiction stems from our ill-conceived idea of the original sin. In earlier times, some people thought the original sin implied 'gluttony,' while others thought it was 'sex.' But as we observed earlier, it is nothing but the acquisition of scientific knowledge.

Now, a child is an offspring of its parents so the human tendency to worship science lies dormant in it. In this sense, child, as a member of the big human family, is the inheritor of the original sin. But small children are free of redeemable sin (1 John 5:16, 17). It is also possible to have people like Nathaniel (Jn. 1:47)—people who are free of redeemable sin.

Cave dwellers, shepherds and those living in far-flung forests and islands were humble people. They had not heard about agriculture, let alone science. In the advanced regions of the world, they were looked down upon by civilised people as "savages." Some of these savages survived the wrath of God (the total destruction of the world), and started rebuilding the earth right from scratch. These people are represented by Cain, the so-called second-born child or son of Adam. It took thousands of years for these savages to fill up the face of the earth. Most of them used their brains and made advancements in education and culture (especially agriculture as represented by Abel) and gradually climbed up the ladder of scientific achievements, leaving others, who were still shepherds (represented by Abel), far behind. The advanced group probably wanted to rule over the entire world. This group must have invaded the countries where the so-called savages were living, and the backward shepherds must have put up a strong resistance. The sense of superiority that the advanced had must have provoked them to use their weapons, and this war must have destroyed human civilsation for the second time. This may be termed as the "Second Adam Cycle."

The survivors of this destruction were some humble and meek cave dwellers, shepherds and people living in far-flung forests and islands. It is written that Cain went to the land of Nod. This type of expulsion from a particular garden or piece of land symbolises extermination of the human race.

Once again, they grew in number, which is represented by Enoch. In this way, each successive name that surfaces is the name of a patriarch representing a particular "Adam Cycle." In this way, the deceptive genealogy records up to the children of Lamech, and then, the continuation is maintained through Seth and so on. The story gives the impression that the so-called generations of Cain and Seth were contemporary, which is not so. In this way, the genealogy recorded in the book of Genesis is not the genealogy in its usual sense but a chronological schedule of Adam Cycles. The successive Adam Cycles recurred till the time of Moses. Paul makes a reference to them: "Nevertheless death reigned from Adam to Moses, even over them that had not sinned after the similitude of Adam's transgression..." (Rom. 5:14). Such a devastation does not spare the lives of animals, birds and plants, even innocent men, and that is why Solomon, the wise, writes "For that which befalleth the sons of men befalleth beasts; even one thing befalleth them: as the one dieth, so dieth the other: yea, they have all one breath, so that a man hath no pre-eminence above a beast..." (Ecc. 3:19).

If this is the case, then it can be figured out that the genealogy of Adam recorded in the book of Genesis is not a genealogy as such. Traditional-minded readers may find this interpretation rather far-fetched. But our analytical approach is based on the maxim, "Let the scripture explain the scripture." We therefore have not incorporated any extra-biblical idea. The idea of Adam Cycles is rooted in the scripture in addition to Solomon's wise saying that "The thing that hath been, it is that which shall be; and that which is done is that which shall be done: and there is no new thing under the Sun. Is there anything whereof it may be said, See, this is new? It hath been already of old time, which was before us. There is no remembrance of former things; neither shall there be any remembrance of things that are to come with those that shall come after." (Ecc. 1:9–11).

The style employed to record the first Adam Cycle is the one that is used to record the successive Cycles. In the case of the first Adam Cycle, the expulsion of man from the garden is most significant; it represents the total destruction of mankind by man himself.

According the Bible, Adam lived for 930 years. This information is irrelevant to us but it expresses the view that mankind continued to live in the world and was not totally extinct. From a handful of survivors of the first man-made destruction, the population grew to fill up the earth, and a section of it, being advanced in science, went on to devastate the earth again.

It shows that the period from Adam to Moses does not represent just the destruction of mankind by flood as depicted in the Bible, but many segments, each segment standing for an Adam Cycle named after a patriarch. This new way of looking at the chain of events as described in the book of Genesis challenges our notion of the uninterrupted continuation of the human race from Adam to Noah and from Noah to Moses. It challenges our notion of the genealogy of Adam and others as well. It also affects our perception of the longevity of each patriarch. A patriarch stands for a particular cycle, and we do not have an understanding of the "time-scale" used by the author. For example, 992 years may stand for 9,320 years or even more. We therefore cannot say for sure that Adam and Eve existed only 6,000 years ago. Our analytical method has enabled us to draw the inference that the first appearance of mankind on earth took place some 1,00,000 years ago or even more. Interestingly, the "reign of death" that Paul talks about could not be properly comprehended by scholars.

Genesis chapter two, verse seven, records that God formed man of the dust of the ground and breathed into his nostrils the 'breath of life' The common belief is that God brought man to life by breathing the "breath of life.' But when God created other lower animals on the fifth and sixth day, He did not breathe the breath of life into their nostrils, but they also live as living creatures, some of them live even longer, showing all signs of life. As a matter of fact, there is no biological difference between man and other animals. So what does the expression "breath of life" mean? When God created other animals on the fifth and sixth day, He created none of them in His image or likeness. That is why man can do things that lower animals cannot. But we can point out that there are many lower animals that are physically stronger than man. There are animals who can run or swim faster and live longer than man. But man has an edge over animals. He owes his superiority to animals to his intellect. His intellect has enabled him to achieve astonishing feats.

The picture of God as painted in the book of Genesis makes God look almost like one of us. We find such a picture in the verse that talks about the destruction of the world by flood: "And it repented the Lord that he had made man on the earth, and it grieved him at his heart." If it is so, then where is God's omniscience? Where is predestination? We can find answers to these questions if we accept the fact that a lot of allegory has been used in the book of Genesis. Perhaps, this is why we get the impression that God is one of us. According to the Bible, God's image is implanted in man. This statement points at man's intellectual capacity, not his spirituality.

"Death," as referred to in the Bible, does not mean physical death. Death is an unavoidable milepost in the journey of our life (save Enoch and Elijah, the legendary figures in the book of Genesis, and II Kings). No one can escape death.

God said to Adam not to eat of the tree of the knowledge of good and evil lest he should die. But the book of Genesis does not say that Adam and Eve suffered physical death immediately after eating the forbidden fruit. So, what kind of death befell Adam and Eve? We must not forget that Adam is not an individual. He represents mankind. And the fruit he ate symbolises acquisition of scientific knowledge, which eventually led to the destruction of mankind. The original sin is nothing but man's involvement with science. Paul said, "For the wages of sin is death... " (Rom. 6:23). Death here stands for mass destruction, not for physical death.

Sin leads to death, but sin may be of different degrees. If for all types of sin the penalty is death, then the penalty will not be in proportion to the sin committed. John says " If any man may see his brother sin a sin, which is not unto death, he shall ask, and he shall give him life for them that sin is not unto death. There is a sin unto death: I do not say that he shall pray for it. All unrighteousness is sin: and there is a sin not unto death." (1 John 5:16-17). It is clear that there are two types of sin: redeemable sin and irredeemable sin, which was committed by the ancients. Only the original sin (or science) leads mankind to mass destruction.

Humans took to science to make their lives more comfortable and enjoyable. Unfortunately, they did not realise that science or the original sin could jeopardise their lives in the long run.

Perhaps, the most beautiful, skilful and monumental application of allegory in the entire Bible is found in the story of the creation of man. So skilfully has the picture been painted, so aptly have the symbols been chosen and employed that for thousands of years people have wondered about the true message hidden in the book of Genesis. Till now, no biblical exegesis has brought forth the real message and profound truth that the book of Genesis contains.

Be that as it may, science misleads us when we get attracted by worldly comfort, pleasure and prosperity, because science deceives us by posing as a great benefactor of man. But it is actually a Frankenstein; it ultimately destroys our world, as it did so many times in the past.

ෙ ෙ

CHAPTER II

God's Hatred for Science

As the story of the sons of Adam goes, Abel became a shepherd while Cain took to agriculture. When God refuses to accept Cain's offering of the first fruit of the ground and accepts Abel's offering of his first-born flock, Cain, in a fit of anger, kills Abel. Then God's wrath comes upon Cain, who is eventually driven out of the land. Cain and Abel are fictitious names. What is significant in this story is Cain's cry: "And Cain said unto the Lord, my punishment is greater than I can bear. Behold, thou hast driven me out this day from the face of the earth; and from thy face shall I be hid" (Gen. 4:13-14). Cain goes to a country called Nod and settles down there. He builds a city and names it after his son Enoch. This simple story contains a profound message, which is so revealing and so convincing. A few survivors (Abel) of the great destruction started multiplying. Some of them remained engaged in non-agricultural activities (shepherds), while members of the other group (Cain) took to all sorts of scientific and research activities (agriculture). In other words, Abel became a shepherd, while Cain became an agriculturist. This event is represented by the killing of Abel and transference of Cain to a place east of Eden (the earth) called Nod. Sceptics may frown at this analysis and wonder what is so wrong about the occupation chosen by Cain, that is, agriculture. He took to a noble activity and toiled hard to earn his living. After all, bread is the mainstay of life. He offered the first crop of his field with utmost sincerity and yet God refused to accept his offering. Cain had his own reasons for getting annoyed with Abel, who performed animal sacrifice. God accepted Abel's offering despite the fact that Abel showed cruelty to animals. And so the story goes. But the real meaning of this story is quite different.

Agriculture is a very noble activity, as it feeds us, clothes us, provides raw materials for many of our industries, promotes trade and commerce and so on. We were hunters for around 15,000 years. So, we did not have access to a steady source of food. It was agriculture that assured us of a steady supply of food. The rise of agriculture also enabled us to devote some of our time to finding ways and means of improving the other spheres of our lives besides gathering food. Modern civilisation owes its root to agriculture. According the Bible, agriculturists looked down upon shepherds. For example, Genesis chapter 46, verses 31–34, tell us how the Israelites had settled in the land of Goshen rather than in Egypt proper because the Egyptians objected to pastoral pursuit. "And Joseph said unto his brethren, and unto his father's house, I will go up, and show Pharaoh, and say unto him, My brethren, and my father's house, which were in the land of Canaan, are come unto me; and the men are shepherds, for their trade hath been to feed cattle; and they have brought their flocks, and their herds, and all that they have. And it shall come to pass, when Pharaoh shall call you, and shall say, What is your occupation? That ye shall say, Thy servants' trade hath been about cattle from our youth even until now, both we, and also our fathers: that ye may dwell in the land of Goshen; for every shepherd is an abomination unto the Egyptians." On the whole, the agricultural type has always represented a higher civilisation. No matter how innocent and benevolent agricultural activities may appear to be, they contain the seed of developed science. During the pastoral stage, there was no need for tools. A stick in the hand was enough to drive the animals from pasture to pasture and a modest stable was enough to keep animals under human care. But agricultural activities demand inventions, production and use of different types of tools. They require the services of miners, blacksmiths, carpenters, etc. The need for mechanised agriculture necessitates designing of better tools, which in turn, calls for mining, metallurgy, etc. Science used for designing and manufacturing these tools is further used for inventing more sophisticated tools, appliances, apparatuses, machines, plants, etc., meant for making our lives more comfortable. The desire to dominate and exploit others soon spurs man to use science for producing dangerous warheads. Eventually, man starts producing nuclear weapons—a Frankenstein is finally born.

Indeed, many bible experts fail to understand why God refused to accept Cain's offering. They blame the Scriptures for favouring shepherds. The story of Cain and Abel is intended to show that shepherds are more virtuous than the ploughmen. That is why God refused to accept Cain's offering. Civilisation rests mainly upon agriculture. Indeed, agriculture is the cradle of developed science, the seed of the poisonous fruit-bearing tree. We can consider this incident as the "Second Adam Cycle."

ೞ ೲ

CHAPTER III

God's Attitude to Trade and Commerce

Another reason why God looks down upon agriculture is that agricultural raw materials contribute towards industrial growth, which is vital for economic prosperity. Agriculture leads to trade and commerce, which have been looked down upon by God.

Why does the Bible consider trade and commerce evil? The Old Testament— especially the prophetic books— vehemently criticises trade and commerce. The book of Ezekiel says: "Now, thou son of man, take up a lamentation for Tyrus; and say unto Tyrus, O thou that art situate at the entry of the sea, which art a merchant of the people for many isles, Thus saith the Lord God; O Tyrus, thou hast said, I am of perfect beauty. Thy borders are in the midst of the seas, thy builders have perfected thy beauty. '' (Ezek. 27:2-4)

God clearly shows the iniquities of man saying: "Tarshish was thy merchant by reason of the multitude of all kind of riches; with silver, iron, tin, and lead, they traded in thy fairs. Javan, Tubal, and Meshech, they were thy merchants: they traded the persons of men and vessels of brass in thy market. They of the house of Togarmah traded in thy fairs with horses and horsemen and mules. The men of Dedan were thy merchants; many isles were the merchandise of thine hand:

they brought thee for a present, horns of ivory and ebony. Syria was thy merchant by reason of the multitude of the wares of thy making: they occupied in thy fairs with emeralds, purple, and broidered work, and fine linen, and coral, and agate. Judah, and the land of Israel, they were thy merchants: they traded in thy market wheat of Minnith, and Pannag, and honey, and oil, and balm. Damascus was thy merchant in the multitude of the wares of thy making, for the multitude of all riches; in the wine of Helbon, and white wool. Dan also and Javan going to and fro occupied in thy fairs: bright iron, cassia, and calamus, were in thy market. Dedan was thy merchant in precious clothes for chariots. Arabia, and all the princes of Kedar, they occupied with thee in lambs, and rams, and goats: in these were they thy merchants. The merchants of Sheba and Raamah, they were thy merchants: they occupied in thy fairs with chief of all spices, and with all precious stones, and gold. Haran, and Canneh, and Eden, the merchants of Sheba, Asshur, and Chilmad, were thy merchants. These were thy merchants in all sorts of things, in blue clothes, and broidered work, and in chests of rich apparel, bound with cords, and made of cedar, among thy merchandise. The ships of Tarshish did sing of thee in thy market: and thou wast replenished, and made very glorious in the midst of the seas. Thy rowers have brought thee into great waters: the east wind hath broken thee in the midst of the seas. Thy riches, and thy fairs, thy merchandise, thy mariners, and thy pilots, thy calkers, and the occupiers of thy merchandise, and all thy men of war, that are in thee, and in all thy company which is in the midst of thee, shall fall into the midst of the seas in the day of thy ruin. The suburbs shall shake at the sound of the cry of thy pilots. And all that handle the oar, the mariners, and all the pilots of the sea, shall come down from their ships, they shall stand upon the land; And shall cause their voice to be heard against thee, and shall cry bitterly, and shall cast up dust upon their heads, they shall wallow themselves in the ashes: and they shall make themselves utterly bald for thee, and gird them with sackcloth, and they shall weep for thee with bitterness of heart and bitter wailing. And in their wailing they shall take up a lamentation for thee, and lament over thee, saying, What city is like Tyrus, like the destroyed in the midst of the sea? When thy wares went forth out of the seas, thou filledst many people; thou didst enrich the kings of the earth with the multitude of thy riches and of thy merchandise. In the time when thou shalt be broken by the seas in the depths of the waters, thy merchandise and all thy company in the midst of thee shall fall. All the inhabitants of the isles shall be astonished at thee, and their kings shall be sore afraid, they shall be troubled in their countenance. The merchants among the people shall hiss at thee; thou shalt be a terror, and never shalt be any more. '' (Ezek. 27:12-36)

God's anger fell upon Tyrus. He decided to wipe it from the map of the world, in the same way as it was destroyed at the time of Adam, at the time of Cain and Abel, at the time of Noah and at the time of the historical Babylon—and it is yet to happen at the time of the prophetical Babylon. There are so many things common between Tyrus and the prophetical Babylon. Enormous wealth accumulation by dint of merchandise makes people proud and arrogant; they start inventing scientific devices that make them almost equal to God.

In the book of Ezekiel , the added information has been recorded as: 'Son of man, say unto the prince of Tyrus, Thus saith the Lord God; Because thine heart is lifted up, and thou hast said, I am a god, I sit in the seat of God, in the midst of the seas ; yet thou art a man, and not God, though thou set thine heart as the heart of God: behold, thou art wiser than Daniel; there is no secret that they can hide from thee: with thy wisdom and with thine understanding thou hast gotten thee riches, and hast gotten gold and silver into thy treasures: By thy great wisdom and by thy traffic hast thou increased thy riches, and thine heart is lifted up because of thy riches: therefore thus saith the Lord God; Because thou hast set thine heart as the heart of God; Behold, therefore I will bring strangers upon thee, the terrible of the nations: and they shall draw their swords against the beauty of thy wisdom, and they shall defile thy brightness. They shall bring thee down to the pit, and thou shalt die the deaths of them that are slain in the midst of the seas. Wilt thou yet say before him that slayeth thee, I am God? but thou shalt be a man, and no God, in the hand of him that slayeth thee. Thou shalt die the deaths of the uncircumcised by the hand of strangers: for I have spoken it, saith the Lord God."(Ezek. 28:2-10)

Profiteering and riches beget pride. What is the outcome of greed and pride?God says, ''Thou hast defiled thy sanctuaries by the multitude of thine iniquities, by the iniquity of thy traffic; therefore will I bring forth a fire from the midst of thee, it shall devour thee, and I will bring thee to ashes upon the earth in the sight of all them that behold thee"(Ezek. 28:18).

It is crystal clear that Tyrus had gone nuclear. It is none but God Himself who would reduce Tyrus to ashes. We therefore consider the incident as the" Third Adam Cycle.''

It is of paramount importance that even Jesus had contempt for trading and merchandise: "And found in the temple those that sold oxen and sheep and doves, and the changers of money sitting : And when he had made a scourge of small cords, he drove them all out of the temple, and the sheep, and the oxen; and poured out the changers' money, and overthrew the tables; And said unto them that sold doves, Take these things hence; make not my Father's house a house of merchandise." (Jn.2:14-16)

The same contempt for trading and merchandise is observed in the book of Revelation where the prophetical Babylon has been described as the chief of trading nations and her activity of trading and other sins have been condemned thoroughly and regarded as the cause of her final destruction (in a prophetic sense). The sin of the prophetical Babylon has been described as "For all nations have drunk of the wine of the wrath of her fornication, and the kings of the earth have committed fornication with her, and the merchants of the earth are waxed rich through the abundance of her delicacies." (Rev.18:3). Again: "And the merchants of the earth shall weep and mourn over her; for no man buyeth their merchandise any more: the merchandise of gold, and silver, and precious stones, and of pearls, and fine linen, and purple, and silk, and scarlet, and all thyine wood, and all manner vessels of ivory, and all manner vessels of most precious wood, and of brass, and iron, and marble, and cinnamon, and odours, and ointments, and frankincense, and wine, and oil, and fine flour, and wheat, and beasts, and sheep, and horses, and chariots, and slaves, and souls of men. And the fruits that thy soul lusted after are departed from thee, and all things which were dainty and goodly are departed from thee, and thou shalt find them no more at all. The merchants of these things, which were made rich by her, shall stand afar off for the fear of her torment, weeping and wailing, and saying, Alas, alas, that great city, that was clothed in fine linen, and purple, and scarlet, and decked with gold, and precious stones, and pearls! For in one hour so great riches is come to nought. And every shipmaster, and all the company in ships, and sailors, and as many as trade by sea, stood afar off, and cried when they saw the smoke of her burning, saying, What city is like unto this great city! And they cast dust on their heads, and cried, weeping and wailing, saying, Alas, alas, that great city, wherein were made rich all that had ships in the sea by reason of her costliness! for in one hour is she made desolate." (Rev. 18:11-19).

It has been pointed out that agriculture, a seemingly innocent science, is responsible for the invention of tools ranging from ordinary appliances to highly developed weapons, such as rockets, missiles and nuclear bombs. Trade and commerce, which are offshoots of agriculture, likewise appear to be innocent and beneficial but ultimately lead to wars between nations.

ೞ ಙ

CHAPTER IV

The Wickedness of Mankind

T he scripture says, "And God saw the wickedness of man was great in the earth, and that every imagination of the thoughts of his heart was only evil continually. And it repented the Lord that he had made man on the earth, and it grieved him at his heart. And the Lord said, I will destroy man whom I have created from the face of the earth; both, man and beasts, and the creeping thing, all the fowls of the air; for it repenteth me that I have made them. But Noah found grace in the eyes of the Lord" (Gen. 6:5 – 8). All that happened during the eve of the universal inundation, during the time of Noah.

What awful things were happening before the flood? Some strange information, indeed, has been given to us—copulation between the sons of God and the daughters of men, the offspring becoming 'mighty' men and the 'men of renown'. Our concept of God, angels, etc., gets shattered by this awful, epic information. The Bible, on the other hand, has not failed to keep us informed that God is spirit and so are the angels (John 4: 24; 2 Cor. 3:17). The daughters of men are, no doubt, in their flesh and blood. This biblical account reads like an epic—the sons of God, who are great spiritual beings, get attracted to the beautiful daughters of men and marry them to produce children, who turn out to be 'mighty men' and 'men of renown.' This episode can be regarded as a scandal surrounding the sons of God, compromising their dignity, bringing them to the level of ordinary men. The biblical account of this happening reads, "And it came to pass, when men began to multiply on the face of the earth, and daughters were born unto them, that the sons of God saw the daughters of men that they were fair; and they took them wives of all which they chose. And the Lord said, My Spirit shall not always strive with man, for that he also is flesh: yet his days shall be a hundred and twenty years. There were giants in the earth in those days; and also after that, when the sons of God came in unto the daughters of men, and they bare children to them, the same became mighty men which were of old, men of renown."(Gen. 6:1-4)

What the author skilfully conveys to us through these biblical verses is that the pious part of our mind is represented by the 'sons of God' and its impious counterpart is represented by the 'daughters of men.' As long as the pious part of our mind remains dominant, we are like the 'sons of God,' but when the impious part of our mind becomes dominant and the pious part becomes dormant, we become like the 'daughters of men.' It is evident that we have both the 'sons of God' and 'daughters of man' in us. But since these two are mutually exclusive as far as their dominion and power over us is concerned, when we act like the 'sons of God', the 'daughters of men' in us are rendered inert and we continue to be the 'sons of God.' But a time comes when the impious part of our mind overshadows the pious part. The pious part of our mind becomes dormant, showing that the logic the impious part is bringing forth is correct. We, by our very nature, follow the dictates of either the pious or impious mind, depending upon which one is more appealing. The biblical verses we are focussing on show that the pious part of their mind could not resist the temptations brought forward by the impious part of their mind. This surrender of domain is represented by the metaphor 'marriage.'

This account records the state of affairs just before the flood. The first destruction has been symbolically represented by the name 'Adam.' It was followed by the second destruction symbolically represented by the names 'Cain and Abel.' Likewise, the successive names that appear (descendants of Adam) stand to represent a clean sweep of the board. This time, the people who survived the universal slaughter did not know anything about science. At this stage, the pious part of their mind dominated. People of those days were the sons of God. But after some time, they reached a stage where the impious part of their mind prompted them to go for agriculture and trade. It made appeals to the pious part of the mind, which somehow agreed. It was in fact the willingness of the pious part of the mind (the sons of God) to yield to the temptation of its impious counterpart (the daughters of men), which is represented by the metaphor 'marriage.'

But why does such a "marriage" kindle the wrath of God? What is wrong with finding ways and means of making life easier and more comfortable? The need for food cannot be neglected by humans at any stage of their development. To the wandering shepherd, agriculture appeared to be too lucrative. But God knew that agriculture, along with its associated evil, trade and commerce, will pave the way for yet another universal slaughter. That was the reason why God disapproved of the subjugation of the pious mind.

The paraphrase of the verses in question should thus read: 'It came to pass that when men began to multiply on the face of the earth, and their worldly desires kept on mounting, they let the impious part of their mind, which pleaded for knowledge or science, subjugate the pious part. It kindled the anger of God. God found that man could not lead a spiritual life for a long period of time and was quick to attend to material needs. Therefore, God shortened the length of the 'Adam Cycle' to 120 years (in His own time-scale) instead of 900 and some odd years. There were great scientists in those days and also afterwards. When men went ahead with scientific inventions and research, many more scientists came into prominence; they were mighty scientists of those days—the renounced people.'

The understanding that the pious part of the human mind has been called 'sons of God' and the impious part 'daughters of men' needs more biblical back-up. When humans lead a simple life and their minds were not infected by strong desires for material prosperity (as was the case of humans at the beginning of the first Adam Cycle), they were the 'sons of God,' but when their more volatile impious mind was awakened to respond to their needs, they became the 'daughters of men.' When the impious part of the mind started to dominate, men drifted towards science and technology and reached a stage where they started competing with God. Man became arrogant, and God was much displeased with the arrogance and wickedness of the impious man. "And God saw that the wickedness of man was great in the earth, and that every imagination of the thoughts of his heart was only evil continually."(Gen.6:5). When humans became increasingly scientific-minded their reverence for God diminished by the same proportion. This inversely proportionate function of "fear of the Lord" and the "promotion of science" is the reason for which God did not approve of their scientific activities.

However, the book of Genesis is not the only book to divide the human mind into its two constituent parts. Jesus and Paul have also done the same. "But love ye your enemies, and do good, and lend, hoping for nothing again; and your reward shall be great, and ye shall be the children of the

Highest..." (Luke 6:35). Again "Jesus answered them, is it not written in your Law, I said Ye are Gods?" (John 10:34) And again, "I have said,' 'You are gods. And all of you are children of the Most High" (Psalm 82:6). But what types of people have been elevated to the status of God? "If He called them gods, to whom the world of God came, and the scripture cannot be broken." (John. 10:35). It implies that God-fearing, pure-hearted people are the "sons of God" On the other hand, Jesus said to some people, "Ye are of your father the devil, and the lusts of your father ye will do" (John. 8:44). When Jesus foretold His death, Jesus rebuked Peter and called him Satan. The scripture says, "And Peter took him, and began to rebuke him. But when he had turned about and looked on his disciples, he rebuked Peter, saying, Get the behind me, Satan: for thou savourest not the things that be of God, but the things that be of men..." (Mark. 8:32, 33).

To get the true and convincing explanation, let us recall three more incidents when Jesus lost touch with God, but immediately re-established the union. Once, after starving for forty days and forty nights, He was led by the spirit to be tempted. The pious part of Jesus' mind had become inert for a while, and the impious part dominated over it. When the impious part of His mind woke up, the pious part of His mind gave a fitting reply to the questions put forward by the impious part. The impious part of His mind said, "...If thou be the Son of God, commend these stones to be made bread." (Matt. 4:3). But Jesus could not be persuaded because of His over-vigilant pious mind and He vexed with the passion for the worldly pleasure and said "...Man shall not live by bread alone, but by every word that proceeds from the mouth of God." (Matt. 4: 4). Here Jesus readily got the quotation from the book of Deuteronomy, a ditto copy of the said verse. Man needs worldly things but these needs are to be kept at a bare minimum, keeping room for spiritual needs.

Then the impious part of His mind took Him to the Holy City, and by sitting on a pinnacle of the temple asked Him, "...If thou be the Son of God, cast thyself down: for it is written, He shall give his angels charge concerning thee: and their hands they shall bear thee up, lest at any time thou dash thy foot against a stone." (Matthew. 4:6). Jesus replied quickly, "It is written again, 'Thou shall not tempt the Lord thy God.'" (Matthew. 4:7).

Again the impious part of His mind took Him to a high mountain and showed Him the world, and the glory of them and said, "All these things I will give thee, if you wilt fall down and worship me" (Matthew 4:9). Then Jesus said to him, "Get thee hence, Satan: for it is written, 'Thou shall worship the Lord thy God, and Him only shall thou serve'" (Matthew 4:10). It was then that the impious part of His mind left Him and the pious part of His mind (angels) came and served Him. Jesus could overcome the situation through the pious part of His mind

This drama was repeated when Jesus, full of agony, prayed incessantly in the garden of Gethsemane to God for the "removal of the cup." For a moment the impious part of His mind made Him pray: "...Father, if thou be willing, remove this cup from me... "(Luke. 22: 42). It was going to jeopardise the entire plan of God for mankind. Jesus, as if unwittingly, tried to escape the inhuman torture and keep mankind unsaved. The next moment He came back to Himself (the pious part of His mind): "And there appeared an angel unto him from heaven, strengthening him" (Luke. 22:43). Quickly, He withdrew the supplication, saying, "...nevertheless not mine will, but thine, be done" (Luke. 22:42).

When Jesus realised that the impious part of his mind had obscured the pious part, He at once screamed, "Eli, Eli, lama sabachthani?" that is, "My god, My God, why hast thou forsaken me?" (Matt. 27:46) This scream did not result from His physical pain. If the robbers could endure the pain of crucifixion, Jesus could do it all the more. It was neither the fear of death, nor the unbearable physical pain that made Him scream. It was the sudden, unforeseen disunion with God — the subjugation of the pious part of His mind — that made Him scream.

It can be said that when men are satisfied with the things provided by God, they are in Eden — a heavenly place. They harness their earthly desires and are, consequently, regarded as "sons of god." But when they are driven by worldly desires, their thoughts revolve around finding ways and means of making their lives more and more comfortable; and so they take refuge in "science." In other words, they become the "daughters of men."

Apostle Paul declares "O wretched man that I am" (Romans 7:24). This is a strange remark by Apostle Paul about himself. It is strange that Apostle Paul whose position is only next to that of Jesus in the New Testament, who had already gone through the process of transformation from Saul to Paul, from cocoon to butterfly, suddenly discovers evil in himself. A spiritually renewed man, who claims, "I am crucified with Christ: nevertheless I live; yet not I, but Christ liveth in me" (Galatians. 2:20), and " I have fought a good fight, I have finished my course, I have kept the faith" (2 Timothy 4: 7). He continues to affirm the fact that the Saul in him is dead and gone and that he is a new person. The promising young man, who had a promising life in front of him, took up the Cross and followed Jesus. He was a spiritually renewed man — a man who forged ahead through all sorts of persecutions; he was a "born-again" believer. The "old man" referred to by him was his own sinful self of the past who died while on his way to Damascus. The person who came to live in his body was the antithesis of his former self. Saul was known for letting loose a reign of terror against the believers in Christ. God's grace transformed him into Paul, the antithesis of Saul. After becoming Paul, he gave up all worldly matters and advised others to follow suit. He said, "For we know that the law is spiritual: but I am carnal, sold under sin. For that which I do I allow not: for what I would, that do I not; but what I hate, that do I. If then I do that which I would not, I consent unto the law that it is good. Now then it is no more I that do it, but sin that dwelleth in me. For I know that in me (that is, in my flesh,) dwelleth no good thing: for to will is present with me; but how to perform that which is good I find not. For the good that I would I do not: but the evil which I would not, that I do. Now if I do that I would not, it is no more I that do it, but sin that dwelleth in me. I find then a law, that, when I would do good, evil is present with me. For I delight in the law of God after the inward man: But I see another law in my members, warring against the law of my mind, and bringing me into captivity to the law of sin which is in my members. O wretched man that I am! who shall deliver me from the body of this death? (Romans 7:14–24)

Unfortunately, no scholar has tried to interpret the abovementioned incident in the light of the dichotomy between the pious and impious parts of the mind.

He has used the first-person pronoun to denote himself and no one else. But the *I* represents only half of his self, that is, the pious part of his mind. This is clear from the line, "For I delight in the law of God after the inward man." The counterpart of his pious mind has been represented by 'sin' and 'flesh.' Apostle Paul was quite aware of the existence of his dual mind, the "inward man" or *I* being the pious part of his mind. But the impious part of his mind is more dominant. Saul, for all practical purposes, had died. But Saul, the old man, had regenerated into a man who is not less than Paul himself. Paul, as we know, is the Paul about whom the book of Acts tells how he used to persecute Christians and how, on his way to Damascus, the amazing vision of Christ changed the course of his life. He had a clear idea of the dual nature of his mind, though he regards the impious mind as 'sin' or 'flesh. He was also aware of the fact that the impious part of his mind was more volatile, more susceptible to strong desires. Not only Paul, but also Jesus could make the pious part of the mind shine like the full moon in the clear autumn sky.

Unfortunately, man cannot make the pious part of the mind dominate the impious part (evil) for a long time. Apostle Paul suggests that efforts need to be made to defeat the impious part of the mind with the spiritual power of the pious part. This is the common thread that runs through most of the teachings of Jesus and His apostles. If we neglect these teachings and allow the impious part of our mind dominate the pious part, we are sure to be punished by God. And the punishment would be nothing less than mass-destruction.

It should, however, be noted that no mass-destruction would take place as long as upright people exist in this world–this is the promise God made to Abraham.

ଓଃ ଓଃ

CHAPTER V

Noah and His Ark

In the days of Noah, God destroyed the world by universal inundation, as man had become scientifically minded and his reverence for God had diminished drastically. The inverse relationship between the 'promotion of science' and the 'fear of the lord' is the reason why God does not approve of man's involvement in science.

Now, about Noah's time, it is written in the Bible, "Then the Lord saw that the wickedness of man was great in the earth, and that every imagination of the thoughts of his heart was only evil, continually" (Gen. 5:6). Let us look at what was going on during the time of Noah and his predecessors. Noah was not the only son of Lamech; he had many brothers and sisters.

There must have been many great scientists during Noah's time and they must have been trying to regulate natural phenomena. God was angry with man, as regulating or tampering with natural phenomena was not within man's domain. God was angry 'for the Lord saw the wickedness of man was great.' This 'wickedness' is suggestive of the highly advanced scientific activities of man. But Noah was part of a group of naive, righteous people who had nothing to do with the scientific advancements taking place during those days.

It is quite likely that God inspired these people to be navigators so that the human race would not become extinct. These navigators needed many animals and birds to be kept in their ships as food for their long voyages.

It was the Holy Spirit that prompted Noah and his people to become navigators. The Bible testifies to this happening. The tribe of Dan occupied two different areas in the Holy Land before the Assyrian captivity. There was a colony on the sea-coast of Palestine. The people there were mainly seamen; it is recorded, "Dan abode in ships." It is also possible that Noah (the righteous people) abode in ships. Animals and birds were their food—that is why God provided them with animals and birds. It holds to reason that the scientists of those days were trying to produce artificial rain. God had tried to prevent them from doing so by sending the prophets to them, but they did not pay any heed to them. The scientists ultimately succeeded in producing artificial rain but could not contain it, hence the worldwide deluge. It is mentioned that it rained for forty days and forty nights till even the highest place on earth was submerged by floodwater. But the righteous people were safe; God's grace kept their ship afloat. These people dismounted from their ship after the floodwater receded, and their descendants spread over the face of the earth. Should we regard this happening as the fourth "Adam Cycle"?

ೞ ಏ

CHAPTER VI

The Historical Babylon

Long time ago, there was a city called Babylon. It was established in 1700 B.C. Located between the rivers Euphrates and Tigris, Babylon was a city-state of ancient Mesopotamia. The kings of Mesopotamia ruled over it for several thousand years. But its boundaries varied from period to period. Babel is the ancient name of the city of Babylon. Babel was one of the three important cities founded by the great warrior, hunter, Nirmod, in the land of Shinar. The other two cities were Erech and Accad.

Enclosed with lofty walls, Babylon was a big city. The early settlers of the city made advancement in several spheres. During the reign of Nebuchadnezzar, Babylon climbed to the peak of civilisation and power, which is known as 'Babylonian civilisation.'

For the first time in human history, brick and mortar were made by the Babylonians. During the reign of Nebuchadnezzar, they rebuilt the city of Babylon brick by brick. They rebuilt the city so that it could become the showpiece of the ancient world. Their crowning achievement was a stupendous tower, whose top reached the heavens. That tower was nothing but the cooling tower of a plutonium-producing reactor, with its pier. The Babylonians had gone nuclear!

They made a big city, which was situated on both sides of the river Euphrates, and the two parts were connected by a stone bridge. On both sides of the bridge was a royal palace. The palaces were connected not only by the stone bridge, but also a tunnel running under the river.

The Babylonians had made three- and four-storeyed houses, and their streets were wide and straight; they intersected approximately at right angles, and were paved with bricks and bitumen. It was a well-planned city—perhaps the best city of ancient times. But the Babylonians rebuilt it as a monument in order to become famous. It was a proud city— the richest city in the world.

God considered it as a rebellious city because it was fraught with arrogance and false pride. The Babylonians had replaced God with science. Scientific discoveries and inventions had become the order of the day. Birds were outnumbered by aeroplanes, missiles, rockets and artificial satellites; fishes were outnumbered by ocean liners, submarines and navel forces; guns and cannons were replaced by nuclear warheads; and the top of the tower was supposed to reach the heavens. So God paid them back in the same coin.

It is allegorically written that God came down from the heaven to see the tower. He came down to confound their language, so that no person could understand what the other person was saying.

"Confound their language" means destruction. God played havoc with the historical Babylon. In other words, the Babylonians themselves destroyed the land of Babylon by nuclear warheads. Only the humble and meek could survive the catastrophe caused by weapons of mass destruction. That was how the Babylonians made atonement for their sins.

Our faith in God seems to be inversely proportional to the knowledge of science. Science and God stand poles apart. Babylon is the pseudo name for the entire world.

So, the world was destroyed for the fifth time. The destruction of the historical Babylon may be termed as the fifth 'Adam Cycle.' The survivors of this destruction were a few cave dwellers, island dwellers, shepherds, etc. The scripture says "Because the Lord did there confound the language of all the earth: and from thence did the Lord scatter them abroad upon the face of the earth" (Gen. 11:9).

ःल ফ

CHAPTER VII

Destruction of Sodom and Gomorrah

"And the Lord said (to Abraham), because the cry of Sodom and Gomorrah is great, and because their sin is very grievous; I will go down now, and see whether they have done altogether according to the cry of it, which is come unto me; and if not, I will know " (Gen. 18: 21, 22).

In the allegorical sense, Abraham started to intercede for Sodom saying peradventure there be fifty righteous people in the city along with the wicked men, will God punish by destroying the city? But the Lord God answered saying, "If I find in Sodom fifty righteous within the city, then I will spare all the place for their sake." So, Abraham was encouraged to strike a balance with the Lord saying, "If there be forty-five righteous people in the city along with the wicked men, will the Lord destroy the city?" The Lord said, "If I find forty-five righteous people, I will not destroy it. Abraham spoke to God yet again and said, "Should there be forty righteous people in the city, will the Lord destroy it? And the Lord answered he would not do it for the forty's sake. Abraham then reduced the number of righteous people to thirty. "If there will be thirty righteous people, will the Lord destroy it?" he asked. God said, "I will not do it, if I find thirty there."

Abraham asked again, "If there will be twenty righteous people, will God destroy it? God answered, "I will not do it for the twenty's sake." Finally, Abraham asked, "If there be just ten people who are righteous, then what will happen?" God answered, "I will not destroy it for the ten's sake." And God went his way.

There was a righteous man named Lot. The Lord had sent a couple of angels to Sodom. And the angels had said to Lot to take his wife and two daughters and flee from the city, as God had decided to destroy it soon. Since the number of Lot and his family fell very much short of ten, the Lord God had every right to destroy Sodom. The Lord God thereby kept his promise to Abraham. Lot and his family were asked "look not behind thee, neither stay thou in all the plain" lest they should also die. And soon after that they heard a deafening sound of high explosion." Then the Lord rained upon Sodom and upon Gomorrah brimstone and fire from the Lord out of heaven; and he overthrew those cities, and all the plain, and all the inhabitants of the cities, and that which grew upon the ground. But his wife looked back from behind him, and she became a pillar of salt" (Gen.19:24, 25, 26).

And Abraham, early in the morning, went to the place where he stood before the Lord God. He looked at Sodom and Gomorrah and there the smoke of the country went up as the smoke of a furnace. Thus Sodom and Gomorrah were reduced to ashes.

Certainly, Sodom and Gomorrah had gone nuclear "… because the cry of Sodom and Gomorrah is great, and because their sin is very grievous" (Gen. 18:20). The people of Sodom and Gomorrah became a victim of the original sin (science)— as if they had eaten the forbidden fruit once again. Sodom and Gomorrah are the code names for the entire world. The

Bible says, "… and he overthrew those cities, and all the plain, and all the inhabitants of the cities, and that which grew upon the ground." These words imply that the Lord God had destroyed the entire world. Lot and his two daughters and Abraham and his family are code names for those who escaped this man-made catastrophe.

The Old Testament says, "And the Lord said, Behold, the man is become as one of us, to know good and evil." (Gen. 3:22) From this verse we learn that God has a dual mind, i.e., 'good' and 'evil'. This is the dichotomy of God's mind. Again, God said, "Let us make man in our image, after our likeness" (Gen.1:26). When God made man, he breathed into his nostrils the 'breath of life, 'brushing aside all the other animals. The 'breath of life' stood for a highly developed brain—a superior brain. Among all living beings only man has been able to rule over the world–thanks to the brain that God gave him.

Jesus said that God can be called *Abba*, which means Father. Jesus is a very big brother of ours, as we are children of God (including Jesus). How true is the saying, 'Like father like son.' Like the mind of God, our mind operates on the principles of 'good' and 'evil.' In other words, the human character embraces both 'thesis' and 'antithesis.'

God gives good things to us for our good. But when He destroys a particular land, say Sodom and Gomorrah, (through scientists), He destroys 'evil,' which is also a part of God.

This happens when a civilisation reaches its zenith. Such things happened in the case of Adam (Gen. 3:8 -13), Cain and Abel (Gen. 4:14), Tyrus (Ezek. 27:2, 3, 4; 28:2, 3), Noah (Gen. 7:17, 18, 19), Babylon (Gen. 11: 7, 8) and Sodom and Gomorrah (Gen. 19:24, 25). During these periods of time, man replaced God with science and, as a result, he had to face the wrath of God

We can regard the destruction of Sodom and Gomorrah as the sixth 'Adam Cycle.'

ભ્ટ બ્ડ

CHAPTER VIII

Prophets' Warning to the Prophetical Babylon

God will Come Down to Destroy Her

"Though Babylon should mount up to heaven, and though she should fortify the height of her strength, yet from me shall spoilers come unto her, saith the Lord" (Jer. 51:53).

Babylon will face the same fate as Lucifer. According to the Bible, Lucifer thought too highly of himself: "How art thou fallen from heaven, O Lucifer, son of the morning! How art thou cut down to the ground, which didst weaken the nations! For thou hast said in thine heart, I will ascend into heaven, I will exalt my throne above the stars of God: I will sit also upon the mount of the congregation, in the sides of the north: I will ascend above the heights of the clouds; I will be like the most High" (Isaiah 14:12-14). Lucifer was cast out of heaven because he had pride in his heart. He was reduced to being a fallen angel. Babylon will suffer the same fate. "For I will rise up against them, saith the Lord of hosts, and cut off from Babylon the name, and remnant, and son, and nephew, saith the Lord." (Isaiah 14:22). Although Babylon fortified the height of her strength, spoilers will come to her to destroy her and the almighty God will stand against her. The sword of Damocles is hanging over her "… for she hath been proud against the Lord, against the holy one of Israel" (Jer. 50:29).

> Make a joyful noise unto the
> Lord, all ye lands.
> Serve the Lord with gladness:
> Come before his presence with singing.
> Know ye that the Lord he is
> God: it is he that hath made us,
> and not we ourselves
>
> (Ps.100: 1-3)

The Book of Psalms says, "It is he that hath made us, and not we ourselves." That is why we should always worship the Lord. But the Babylonians had followed Adam (mankind), who was like an angel. God had commanded Adam not to eat the fruit of the knowledge of good and evil. In other words, God had wanted Adam (mankind) to keep away from science. The historical Babylon had followed in the footsteps of Adam, and the prophetical Babylon has emulated the historical Babylon. While extolling science, the prophetical Babylon has forgotten the fact that science is the creation of the Omnipotent God and that He would descend upon the earth to destroy it.

Reap the Harvest of Sin

"For her sins have reached unto heaven, and God had remembered her iniquities." (Rev. 18:5)

"… for her judgement reacheth unto heaven, and is lifted up even to the skies." (Jer. 51:9)

The prophetical Babylon has committed unpardonable sins—so much so that if its sins were piled up, the top of the pile would reach the heavens. It has displeased God by glorifying science. Therefore, the almighty God will pay it back in the same coin. It would reap the harvest of its sins.

Nations will Cry over Babylon

"Therefore hear ye the counsel of the Lord, that he hath taken against Babylon; and his purposes, that he hath purposed against the land of the Chaldeans: Surely the least of the flock shall draw them out: surely he shall make their habitation desolate with them. At the noise of the taking of Babylon the earth is moved, and the cry is heard among the nations."(Jer. 50:45-46)

"And a mighty angel took up a stone like a great millstone, and cast it into the sea, saying, Thus with violence shall that great city Babylon be thrown down, and shall be found no more at all." (Rev. 18:21)

It is the divine appeal to uproot the land of the Chaldeans, to smash the prophetical Babylon. The nations cry hard because it is the sole supplier of foreign aid. But, ultimately, it became so proud of its capability that it tried to hoodwink even God. The almighty God will punish her for her iniquities.

God Is Against Her

"Behold, I am against thee, O thou most proud, saith the Lord God of hosts: for the day is come, the time that I will visit thee." (Jer. 50:31)

God is against Babylon. Who can save her? The Lord God has seen the iniquity she has committed, her sins have reached unto heaven. Babylon has been too proud; she wants to rule over the earth. So, God warns her saying 'I will visit thee.'

Tit for Tat

"I have laid a snare for thee, and thou art also taken, O Babylon, and thou wast not aware: thou art found, and also caught, because thou hast striven against the Lord. The Lord hath opened his armoury, and hath brought forth the weapons of his indignation: for this is the work of the Lord God of hosts in the land of the Chaldeans." (Jer. 50:24-25)

The Lord says through Jeremiah that he has trapped Babylon, for which, he has laid a snare. Without her knowledge, she has been trapped. Babylon was found guilty of her misdeeds. She put up a fight against the Lord, so the Lord will put up a greater fight against her.

As you Sow, So shall you Reap

"I have spread out my hands all the day unto a rebellious people, which walketh in a way that was not good, after their own thoughts" (Isaiah 65:2).

Right from the days of Adam (mankind), the Lord has been punishing rebellious people. In the beginning, when mankind (Adam) forsook God and went for science, God destroyed mankind. The second victim was Cain, and the third victim was Tyrus; then the earth was deluged by a flood. The fifth victim was the historical Babylon, and the sixth victim was Sodom and Gomorrah. Unfortunately, today's world is also inching towards total annihilation with all its nuclear stockpiles.

A Substitute God

The Bible says, " When ye have transgressed the covenant of the Lord your God, which he commanded you, and have gone and served other gods, and bowed yourselves to them; then shall the anger of the Lord be kindled against you, and ye shall perish quickly from off the good land which he hath given unto you."(Joshua 23:16).

That horrible path has been trodden by Babylon—the wicked path of transgressing the covenant of God. The

Almighty will take His revenge. The anger of the Lord has been kindled against her for she has chosen another God (science). Her peril is at the door. The good land that the Lord has given her will be ruined.

Scientific Knowledge Is a Frankenstein

"...For it is the land of graven images, and they are mad upon their idols" (Jer. 50:38).

Modern (the prophetical) Babylon is worshipping science (idolater) only. Instead of worshipping God Babylon has found a substitute for Him. Science provides worldly pleasure, comfort and prosperity. Apparently, its goodness is beyond any measure. It gives us agriculture so that we can have a steady supply of food. We are better off than men were in the hunting stage. It gives us motor cars, railways, aeroplanes, electricity, telephones and so forth. But a time comes when science shows its true colours. It starts from guns, cannons and all sorts of weaponry but it does not stop there; it goes on to Atom bombs, Hydrogen bombs, Nitrogen bombs and so on. The prophetical Babylon, in particular, and the world, in general, owes everything to science (idols).

Her Doomsday Is Near

"Because the Lord hath spoiled Babylon, and destroyed out of her great voice; when her waves do roar like great waters, a noise of their voice is uttered "(Jer. 51:55). Babylon has a commanding voice because she is economically strong and rules over the people of the earth. The Lord has witnessed her wicked ways and so her destruction is at the door. Soon, she will see her doomsday. The countdown has begun. After her destruction, there will not be any trace of humans. Their houses will be full of doleful creatures, and owls, and wild beasts of the island, and dragons will roam about in the length and breadth of Babylon. She will never be inhabited by men.

The Queen will Be Reduced to Ashes

"How much she hath glorified herself, and lived deliciously" (Rev. 18:7).

The woman representing Babylon has been called a 'whore', which is a symbol of one who stands 'contrary to the scriptures.' It is a prophetical expression.

When John saw her in a vision, he saw the great whore sitting upon many waters. He saw the woman arrayed in purple scarlet colour and decked with gold and precious stones and pearls, having a golden cup in her hand. Indeed, the woman representing Babylon lived a luxurious life. When John saw such a vision, he was wonderstruck. But many of the prophets had foretold about her predicament.

Loss of Children and Widowhood Awaits Her

The Bible says, "...for she saith in her heart, I sit queen, and am no widow, and shall see no sorrow " (Rev. 18:7)." And thou saidst, I shall be a lady for ever: so that thou didst lay these to thy heart, neither didst remember the latter end of it. Therefore hear now this, thou that art given to pleasures, that dwellest carelessly, that sayest in thine heart, I am, and none else beside me, I shall not sit as a widow, neither shall I know loss of children: But these two things shall come to thee in a moment in one day, the loss of children and widowhood: they shall come upon thee in their perfection for the multitude of thy sorceries, and for the great abundance of thine enchantments" (Isaiah 47:7-9).

She keeps telling herself that she is queen. The world regards her as a queen. She is a queen indeed, extending her boundaries all over the earth. The waters on which she is seated, symbolise nations, peoples, races and languages (Rev. 17:15). By dint of her riches she has absolute command over all the nations, people of the earth, all the races and all languages. Moreover, she thinks that she is not a widow, or a weak woman. She has the necessary weaponry to defend herself. Also, she says to herself, I will never know grief. She has too high an opinion of herself. But one day she will be struck with plagues, diseases and grief. The kings, who enriched themselves by obeying her, will weep when they see the smoke billowing from the flames consuming her. The enemy will make its move when she is weak and helpless. God will take vengeance on her.

Judgement will Come in One Hour

"Standing afar off for the fear of her torment, saying, Alas, alas, that great city Babylon, that mighty city! for in one hour is thy judgement come " (Rev. 18:10)

"For in one hour so great riches is come to naught. And every ship master, and all the company in ships, and sailors, and as many trade by sea, stood afar off, And cried when they saw the smoke of her burning, saying what city is like unto this great city! And they cast dust on their heads, and cried weeping and wailing, saying, Alas, alas, that great city, where in were made rich all that had ships in the sea by reason of her costliness ! for in one hour is she made desolate" (Rev. 18: 17-19).

The great city is extremely rich. But as Jesus says, "... verily I say unto you, That a rich man shall hardly enter into the kingdom of heaven. And again I say unto you, it is easier for a camel to go through the eye of a needle, than for a rich man to enter into the kingdom of God" (Matt. 19:23-24). Moreover, she gives aid to foreign nations. She made the earth drunken (foreign aid), the nations have consumed her wine (monetary help). Therefore, the nations are mad (eradicated sovereignty). She has been waiting for the hour to be judged by God and be reduced to ashes.

Her Riches will Be Worthless

"Behold, I shall stair up the Medes against them, which shall not regard silver: and as for gold, they shall not delight in it" (Isaiah 13:17).

"They shall cast their silver in the streets, and their gold shall be removed: their silver and gold shall not be able to deliver them in the day of the wrath of the Lord: they shall not satisfy their souls, neither fill their bowels: because it is the stumbling block of their iniquity" (Ezek. 7:19).

Babylon has got a lot of riches. People of this world will come down on their knees in order to have those riches. But the Lord God will stair up the Medes against them and they will all be prepared to do away with their riches. Silver and gold will not be able to deliver them from the wrath of God, because they are branded as 'ungodly.' They will not be able to satisfy their souls or bowels—this is not annihilation or cessation of being; it is eternal, conscious punishment; Babylonians or men of this world had gone for science and will never repent for the sin they have committed—for their city (the world) will be incinerated.

Her Mother shall Be Ashamed

"Your mother shall be sore confounded; she that bare you shall be ashamed..." (Jer. 50:12)

'Your mother' denotes another nation. So far as the prophetical Babylon is concerned, she was the offspring of another nation. How wonderful is the idea! She that bare you shall be ashamed, after the great holocaust. The word 'mother' is an image. Rather frightful calamities are going to happen to this city, for which the mother should be astonishingly depressed. She is a real mother; a real mother is always concerned about the security and wellbeing of her child. She also worries about the future of the child.

An in-depth study reveals that God had promised Abraham that his descendents will be wealthy, prosperous and powerful and will become a great nation. God's promise was fulfilled partly in Joseph, who went down to Egypt and became a prosperous man. More so, the descendants of Joseph were destined to become more prosperous and more powerful than Joseph. God had translated His blessings many times more in Joseph's sons, Ephraim and Manasseh. Once upon a time Israel was under the Yoke of Assyria. The Israelites were pushed inside Assyria as captives. Down the south, Judah was conquered by Nebuchadnezzar of Babylon. The people of Judah also came to Babylon as captives, including Jeremiah, the prophet. After spending a few years in exile, Jeremiah was free to go to his country. Soon after, he met the Israelites.

Under the leadership of Jeremiah, Israel went to the north-west of Europe; they landed at Ireland, and the name of the place was Ulster. An astonishing fact is that with them were the princess daughter of an eastern king named Tea-Tephi. Once again, the Hebrew princess was married to the prince named Herremon. And the same dynasty continued unbroken; through all the kings of Ireland; was overturned and transplanted again in Scotland; again overturned and moved to England, where the same dynasty continues today.

Down the ages, the descendants of Ephraim and Manasseh were inhabitants of Great Britain. Then the unknown country of America was discovered. With this discovery Manasseh had sailed to New England (America) and Ephraim stayed on in Great Britain.

In this case, 'mother' denotes Great Britain, and Great Britain alone.

A city that was famous for her foreign aid, being the strongest and richest nation of the world, has ended, and her mother should be ashamed.

A Mini World

"And he saith unto me, The waters which thou sawest, where the whore sitteth, are peoples, and multitudes, and nations, and tongues." (Rev. 17:15)

The word 'whore' stands for the one who defies the 'rules' or stands 'contrary to the scripture.' Even Jerusalem and Israel have been referred to as 'whore'. It is a prophetical symbol. ([for Jerusalem] Ezek 16:15-17, 22, 26, 28, 30, Jer. 13:27; [for Israel], Hosea 1:2; 2:2, 4; 4:12, etc.)

The prophetical Babylon has to be cosmopolitan in character. People belonging to different nations are supposed to go over to Babylon and live there. "...and upon all the mingled people that are in the midst of her..." (Jer. 50:37). It implies that it is a cosmopolitan city. It is, as if, a 'mini -world', which constitutes the prophetical Babylon. Different nations have been represented in the prophetical Babylon.

A Newly Created Nation will Be Destroyed

"...behold, the hindermost of the nations shall be a wilderness, a dry land, and a desert." (Jer. 50:12)

The youngest of the nations, the hindermost of the nations and newborn of the nations—what is there in store for her? There will be a holocaust in the city. The tall buildings of the city will collapse one after another. The entire city will be in flames. It will become a dry land, for the Lord says (through Jeremiah), "A drought upon her waters; and they shall be dried up" (Jer. 50:38). The city will be transformed to a desert. It will be a sea of sands with no vegetation. Its soil will be full of stones and salt, with nettles, thorns and thistles. It will consist of waterless wastes, inhabited by horrible beasts such as serpents, scorpions, owls, porcupines, wild asses, jackals, ostriches and ravens. Out of it will come the fiery, all-consuming storm and not the mild wind that brings rain and fertility. It will be a land the essence of which is disorder and confusion, the wilderness.

She will Be Attacked from the North

"For lo, I will raise and cause to come up against Babylon an assembly of great nations from the North country: and they shall set themselves in array against her; from thence she shall be taken; their arrows shall be as of a mighty expert man; none shall return in vain. And Chaldia shall be a spoil: all that spoil her shall be satisfied, saith the Lord" (Jer 50:9, 10).

"Then the heaven and the earth, and all that is therein, shall sing for Babylon: for the spoilers come unto her from the north, saith the Lord." (Jer. 51:48).

"Rejoice over her, thou heaven, and ye holy apostles and prophets: for God hath avenged you on her" (Rev. 18:20).

"I have commanded my sanctified ones, I have also called my mighty ones for mine anger, even them that rejoice in my highness. The noise of a multitude in the mountains, like as of a great people, a tumultuous noise of the kingdoms of nations gathered together: the Lord of hosts mustereth the host of the battle. They come from a far country, from the end of heaven, even the Lord, and the weapons of his indignation, to destroy the whole land." (Isaiah 13:3-5)

Babylon will be attacked from the northern side. It will be attacked by an assembly of great nations. It is perhaps the erstwhile Soviet Russia. In the erstwhile Soviet Union, in Asiatic Russia, there is an Assembly of Muslim nations. Perhaps they would launch the attack. Or perhaps the North Koreans will be launching their first attack. It will be a nuclear war, no doubt, because in the Book of Jeremiah it is written, 'Their arrows (missiles) shall be as of a mighty expert man; none shall return in vain.' Their volley of arrows is so accurate that each arrow will hit the target. In other words, the enemy's nuclear weapons would invariably hit the target. The enemy will be victorious in the war. This has been mentioned particularly: 'all that spoil her shall be satisfied.' Can God's attack on a country be resisted by all other countries put together? NO. It is the almighty God who has created the universe; nothing can go wrong with Him. The almighty God had destroyed the prophetical Babylon before the creation of the earth; of course, it would come to pass in the immediate future.

She Sits upon Many Waters

"O thou that dwellest upon many waters, abundant in treasures, thine end is come, and the measure of thy covetousness" (Jer 51:13).

"...I will shew unto thee the judgment of the great whore that sitteth upon many waters" (Rev. 17:1)

"It was planted in a good soil by great waters, that it might bring forth branches and that it might bear fruit, that it might be a goodly vine." (Ezek. 17:8)

Babylon is located upon many waters. It is an island. Also, she is like a gold mine. Therefore, all nations of the earth are attracted to it. Her merchants are gold diggers. That is why all sorts of people dwell upon her. As for her, she continues to be avaricious. But alas, her days are numbered. The end time is at hand. The countdown has begun. The great city will soon be in flames.

Goods Produced by her will Lose their Exchange Value

"And the merchants of the earth shall weep and mourn over her; for no man buyeth their merchandise any more: The merchandise of gold, and silver, and precious stones, and of pearls, and fine linen, and purple, and silk and scarlet, and all thine wood, and all manner vessels of ivory, and all manner vessels of most precious wood, and of brass and iron, and marble, and cinnamon, and odours and ointments, and frankincense, and wine and oil and fine flour, and wheat, and beasts, and sheep, and horses and chariots, and slaves, and soul of men. And the fruits that thy soul lusted after are departed from thee, and all things which were dainty and goodly are departed from thee, and then shall find them no more at all. The merchants of these things, which were made rich by her, shall stand afar off for fear of her torment, weeping and wailing, And saying, Alas, alas, that great city, that was clothed in fine linen, and purple, and scarlet and decked with gold, and precious stones, and pearls! For in one hour so great riches is come to naught..." (Rev. 18:11-17).

"Neither their silver nor their gold shall be able to deliver them in the day of the Lord's wrath, but the whole land shall be devoured by the fire of his jealousy: for he shall make even a speedy riddance for all them that dwell in the land." (Zeph. 1:18).

The great city shall be no more; her merchants from all over the earth shall weep and mourn for her, because she has been incinerated. All her precious things will be in flames. The radioactive particles in the air will annihilate the people of the island. One press of the button would put the city on fire. The prophet Zephaniah also saw a speedy riddance of the entire land. And their riches will not be able to deliver them in the day of the Lord's wrath and the entire land shall be devoured by fire. Mushroom-like smoke will rise in the sky.

She will Be Incinerated

"Therefore shall her plagues come in one day, death, and mourning, and famine, and she shall be utterly burned with fire; for strong is the Lord God who judgeth her. And the kings of the earth, who have committed fornication and lived deliciously with her, shall bewail her, and lament for her, when they shall see the smoke of her burning, standing afar off for the fear of her torment, saying, Alas, alas, the great city Babylon, that mighty city! for one hour thy judgement come." (Rev. 18:8-10)

Poor Babylon will be incinerated. Death (mass-death) is in store for her; the nuclear weapons will char her soil. And the leaders (kings) of the nations who have received foreign aid and monetary help (fornication) from her will lament for her on seeing smoke billowing from the houses and the factories. The leaders will be very sorry for getting her burnt in fire.

No One can Help it
"...Let now the astrologers, the stargazers, the monthly prognosticators, stand up, and save thee from these things that shall come upon thee. Behold, they shall be as stubble; the fire shall burn them; they shall not deliver themselves from the power of the flame: There shall not be a coal to warm it, nor fire to sit before it." (Isaiah 47:13, 14)

The almighty God says through Isaiah that no one could save the situation. No one could help it. And no one could resist it. The wrath of God will surely come upon Babylon. God shall burn it by fire. No astrologers, no stargazers, no monthly prognosticators will be able to rescue them; the fire shall consume all of them. If the almighty God stands against Babylon, who can save her?

The Great City will Split into Three Parts
"...and thunders, and lightnings, and there was a great earthquake, such as was not since men were upon the earth, so mighty an earthquake, and so great. And the great city was divided into three parts and cities of all nations fell: and great Babylon came in remembrance before God, to give unto her the cup of the wine of the fierceness of his wrath. And

every island fled away and the mountains were not found. And there fell upon men a great hail out of heaven, every stone about the weight of a talent: and men blasphemed God because of the plague of the hail; for plague thereof was exceedingly great. "(Rev. 16:18-21)

The great city will be divided into three parts. But what about us? If a nuclear war breaks out, it is expected that the warring nations will immediately be attacked by rockets and ballistic missiles. It is possible to get some enemy rockets and ballistic missiles destroyed but the remaining few will be enough to wipe out the cities. How many cities are there on earth? If you define a city as having more than 100,000 people in it, there are only 2,300 cities on the planet. (Carl Sagan, *Reversing the Nuclear Arms Race* p 168).

Within seven decades, the globe has put on a dangerous, monster-like attire. In a little more than half a century she has dressed herself as a monster. We have been booby trapped by our nuclear weapons. But the said weapons can be used once and for all. A nuclear war will be an 'omnicide.' It will be a conflict, but also the annihilation of human civilisation. The prophetical Babylon may be the first target, but it does not mean that we will be spared. It will be a difference of days only; '... and cities of all nations fell ' carries a significant verse in the Bible. It includes all the cities of the world. Here John writes in a symbolic way that every house (island) and skyscraper (mountain) will be destroyed because of the nuclear war (hail). Solomon, the wise, writes that "there is no remembrance of former things" (Eccl. 1:11). It implies that what happened in the former Adam Cycle cannot be carried over to the next Adam Cycle owing to the absence of the intelligentsia.

If a nuclear war breaks out, everything for us would be over. At one stroke the entire Babylonian civilisation would be wiped out. Therefore, men of the next Adam Cycle will not know that such a civilisation ever existed.

The sun will rise to see very few people, perhaps half-naked, perhaps yet to learn about agriculture. They would perhaps be eating wild roots, fruits and meat and drinking milk of animals, as the world would not have civilised people.

Will Some People Escape the Catastrophe?

"I heard another voice from heaven, saying, Come out of her, my people, that ye be not partakers of her sins, and that ye receive not her plagues." (Rev. 18:4)

And in the Old Testament it is written, "Go ye forth of Babylon, flee ye from the Chaldians, with a voice of singing declare ye, tell this, utter even to the end of the earth, say ye, The Lord hath redeemed his servant Jacob." (Isaiah 48: 20)

"Flee out of the midst of Babylon, and deliver every man his soul: be not cut off in her iniquity; for this is the time of the Lord's vengeance; I will render unto her a recompense" (Jer. 51:6).

Is there any room for the righteous people for atonement? Yes, there is. There is a clarion call for the people who are tall in faith and righteous to come out of the prophetical Babylon. There is a heavenly call to redeem them so that they may receive the blessings of the Son of God. There is a heavenly call to depart from Babylon so that they may not be counted as partakers of her sins and receive her plagues.

CB BO

Chapter IX

Discovery of the Prophetical Babylon

The historical Babylon stood between the rivers Tigris and Euphrates. But where is the prophetical Babylon? It is the 'city that never sleeps', the city of New York (especially Manhattan) in particular and the United States of America in general. Many Bible scholars, theologians and believers believe that the prophetical Babylon or the modern Babylon is the city of Rome, the city of seven hills. Let us consider the symbols, particularly the arithmetical number 'seven.' The number seven symbolises perfection or a divine number or the complete number. This is why the Book of Revelation talks about 'seven churches,' 'seven spirits,' etc. In the footnote of *The First Scofield Reference Bible*, chapter 18, verse 2, 'Babylon' has been referred to be as 'Rome'. Again in the word list of the *Good News New Testament*, TEV, it is written, "In 1 Peter 5:13 and Revelation, the name Babylon probably refers to the city of Rome." The book, *Bible Lessons on the Book of Revelation* regards Rome as the prophetical Babylon (chapters XIII, XVI, XVII, XVIII and XIX).

According to the Bible, "...The seven heads are the seven mountains, on which the woman sitteth." (Rev. 17:9). This is the vision that John saw. Like all other biblical texts, this vision should not be interpreted literally—something that many Bible scholars have done. We must remember that the Bible is a God-inspired book written by some God-inspired people or prophets who wrote it in the presence of the Holy Spirit, in a trance-like state. Prophet Ezekiel writes "And the spirit entered into me when he spake unto me, and set me on my feet, that I heard him that spake to me" (Ezek. 2:2). The writer of Revelation, John, writes, "I was in spirit on the Lord's day, and heard being behind me a great voice, as of a trumpet, saying, I am Alpha and Omega, the first and the last: and, what thou seest, write in a book, and send it unto the seven churches which are in Asia..." (Rev. 1:10, 11). Before we start interpreting a biblical text, we should try to understand the tone and mood of the writer.

The United States is the only nation that can be regarded as the prophetical Babylon, as it is the richest and most powerful country in the world. It is the world's largest arms manufacturer and exporter. America spends billions of dollars on defence and has the largest number of military bases, the largest fleet and the biggest nuclear arsenal. Rome has neither the wealth nor the military might that America possesses. So the United States of America, or more specifically, Manhattan, is the prophetical Babylon.

CB&EO

Chapter X

Historical Babylon and Prophetical Babylon: Similarities and Differences

Similarities

(1) Both are the richest places of the world. Rebuilding Babylon required an enormous amount of wealth. It was a wonderful city; but the people inhabiting it also made a huge tower in it, which bespoke of their arrogance. The prophetical Babylon is also wealthy and arrogant.

In both the 'Babylons' people wallow in money. The prophetical Babylon's hand is just like the philosopher's stone—capable of turning things into gold. New York is the most prosperous city in the world. This great city controls the entire world with its economic power. The New York money market is the number one money market in the world followed by the London money market.

(2) Like the historical Babylon, the prophetical Babylon has engaged a good number of scientists. People of the historical Babylon had rebuilt a marvellous city. This city was a planned city. Many architects were employed to rebuild it. Also, they had built up a tower—nothing short of the cooling tower of a plutonium-producing reactor. They must have employed a good number of scientists to

make the aforesaid tower.

The prophetical Babylon runs parallel to the historical Babylon. The United States of America is the first country that went nuclear. It could manage to do so mainly because it had many efficient and top-ranking scientists. This is why the prophetical Babylon is in deep waters.

People in both the places found themselves on the highest rung of scientific knowledge. When the world was in the dark, the Babylonians were the first to manufacture brick. They were sharp enough to rebuild the city—a beautiful planned city, a first-of-its-kind city in the whole world. It was the largest city in the world covering 100sq miles. Like the historical Babylon, Manhattan is known for its splendour and architectural glory—its skyscrapers. In order to build these skyscrapers, hundreds of architects must have put their minds together and worked for years together.

Secondly, New York was a Dutch colony. From their humble beginnings they made up the city brick by brick, and it eventually became the largest city in America and one of the largest cities in the world.

Thirdly, New York City (especially Manhattan) facing the Atlantic Ocean, was smaller than what it is now, but the scientists, by dint of their scientific knowledge, enlarged the land area.

(4) The historical Babylon was rebuilt during Nebuchadnezzar's rule. The rebuilding of the new city was followed by the building of the famous Babylonian tower. So, we can say that Nebuchadnezzar was born with a silver spoon in his mouth. The architects made a wonderful city and so we can say that the scientists who made the tower were born with silver spoons in their mouths.

The same happened in the prophetical Babylon. The architects who made the skyscrapers were born with silver spoons in their mouths. The scientists who were responsible for turning the U.S.A into the first nuclear power in the world were born with silver spoons in their mouths. And the scientists who were engaged in the enlargement of the land area of New York City were born with silver spoons in their mouths.

(5) Like the historical Babylon, the prophetical Babylon would be destroyed by fire caused by nuclear bombs. Jeremiah, the prophet, predicted: "Babylon is suddenly fallen and destroyed..." (Jer. 51:8). He also says, "O thou that dwellest upon many waters, abundant in treasures, thine end is come..." (Jer. 51:13). Certainly, it was nuclear war that destroyed the historical Babylon; the prophetical Babylon would be destroyed in a similar manner.

(6) Both are very large places. The historical Babylon was as large as Nineveh. "...Nineveh was an exceedingly great city of three days' journey" (Jonah 3:3); the city was well spread-out on both sides of the river Euphrates. The historical Babylon covered an area of more than 100 sq. miles.

The same happened to the prophetical Babylon. It is the largest city in the U.S.A. Manhattan lies at the core of the economic and cultural playground of the country. Its metropolitan area is 1,384 sq. miles.

(7) Both the cities had similar modes of transportation. For the historical Babylon, the city extended on both sides of the Euphrates. The two parts were connected together by a stone bridge. On both sides of the bridge was a royal palace. How wonderfully were these palaces connected by a tunnel running beneath the river!

Surprisingly, the same type of transport is seen in the prophetical Babylon (Manhattan). Concrete bridges on the East River, such as Brooklyn Bridge, Manhattan Bridge and Williamsburg Bridge, connect Manhattan with Brooklyn. The Queensboro Bridge connects Manhattan with Queens. But the most amazing thing is the tunnel named Midtown Tunnel. There are also a couple of tunnels underneath, named Holland Tunnel and Lincoln Tunnel, to connect with New Jersey. Interestingly, both the historical Babylon and the prophetical Babylon have the same type of transport.

(8) Both the cities went nuclear. The Babylonians made a tower, which was nothing but a cooling tower of a plutonium-producing reactor. That is why " the Lord came down to see the city and the tower, which the children of men builded." (Gen. 11:5). It is clear that the historical Babylon had gone nuclear. They had made nuclear bombs. So, God had to come down to destroy the historical Babylon.

The prophetical Babylon suffers the same fate. America is the first country in the world that went nuclear.

(9) The historical Babylon was completely destroyed. All its inhabitants were gone after the holocaust. According to Genesis 11:9, "…and from thence did the Lord scatter them abroad upon the face of the earth." The historical Babylon continues to be a dead city.

After its destruction, the prophetical Babylon, cries the prophet Isaiah, " will never be inhabited, neither shall it be dwelt in from generation to generation: neither shall the Arabian pitch tent there; neither shall the shepherd make their fold there. But wild beasts of the desert shall lie there; and their houses shall be full of doleful creatures; and owls shall dwell there, and satyrs shall dance there.

And the wild beasts of the islands shall cry in their desolate houses, and dragons in their pleasant palaces: and her time is near to come, and her days shall not be prolonged." (Isaiah 13:20-22)

In his vision, John, the apostle and prophet saw: "And the voice of the harpers, and musicians, and of pipers, and trumpeters, shall be heard no more at all in thee; and no craftsman, of whatsoever craft he be, shall be found any more in thee; and the sound of millstone shall be heard no more at all in thee; And the light of a candle shall shine no more at all in thee; and the voice of the bridegroom and of the bride shall be heard no more at all in thee: for thy merchants were the great men of the earth; for by the sorceries were all nations deceived" (Rev. 18:22, 23).

(10) Again, both the historical Babylonians and the prophetical Babylonians had sharp politicians to guide them. The Bible says nothing about 'politicians' but we can presume that the historical Babylonians had reached the peak of civilisation in those days, which implies that the existing 'intelligentsia' was backed by a sound political system. During the reign of Nebuchadrezzar, a host of 'politicians' gave Nebuchadrezzar political counsel. In 605 B.C., the armies of Babylon under the able leadership of Nebuchadrezzar conquered Egypt and Judah. Before returning to Babylon, Nebuchadrezzar appointed a Jewish official as governor of those who remained in Judah. This political move shows that the king of the historical Babylon had a band of politicians to assist him.

The prophetical Babylon directly or indirectly controls the activities of the rest of the world. But let us take a look at how John, the apostle and the prophet, remarked: "And the woman which thou sawest is that great city, which reigneth over the kings of the earth" (Rev. 17:18). The prophetical Babylon is part and parcel of America.

(11)The historical Babylon had forsaken God. She defied God and embraced science. The Babylonians forgot that science was also God's creation. Therefore, God decided to punish Babylon.

Although the prophetical Babylon has spent a lot on defence, her military might is 'nothing' in the sight of God. Jeremiah proclaimed: "A sword is upon their horses, and upon their chariots, and upon all the mingled people that are in the midst of her; and they shall become as women: a sword is upon her treasures; and they shall be robbed" (Jer 50:37, 38). She thinks her defence is quite strong; "therefore shall her plagues come in one day, death and mourning, and famine; and she shall be utterly burned with fire: for strong is the God who judgeth her" (Rev. 18: 8).

The prophetical Babylon is following in the footsteps of the historical Babylon.

(12)During the time of the historical Babylon, the Babylonians invented brick and slime. To become famous, they used these inventions for making a huge city and a tower. The prophetical Babylon is also known for her amazing inventions.

(13)Like the historical Babylon, the prophetical Babylon is at the zenith of its socio-political and economic power. It is the most powerful nation on earth.

Differences

(1) The historical Babylon no longer exists; the prophetical Babylon is yet to be destroyed.

(2) The historical Babylon was founded by Nirmod, the great warrior-hunter. It was located between the rivers

Euphrates and Tigris on the bank of Mesopotamia. The prophetical Babylon is located away from Mesopotamia.

(3) The historical Babylon is known as "mother Babylon" while the prophetical Babylon is known as "daughter Babylon." Jeremiah, the prophet, speaks to this daughter: Your mother shall be sore confounded; she that bare you shall be ashamed..." (Jer. 50:12).

Jeremiah once again says, "For thus saith the Lord of hosts, the God of Israel; the daughter of Babylon is like a threshing floor, it is time to thresh her: yet a little while, and the time of her harvest shall come." (Jer. 51:33) About the prophetical Babylon, it is said, "O daughter of Babylon, who art to be destroyed." (Ps. 137:8)

Isaiah, the prophet, says, "Come down, and sit on the dust, O virgin daughter of Babylon, sit on the ground: there is no throne; O daughter of Chaldians: for thou shalt no more be called tender and delicate" (Isaiah 47:1).

Zechariah, the prophet, declares: "Deliver thyself, O Zion, that dwellest with the daughter of Babylon" (Zech. 2:7).

(4) According to the Bible, during the period of the historical Babylon, the earth was of one language and speech, but people of the prophetical Babylon speak in many different languages.

(5) During the time of the historical Babylon, the Babylonians were the first to invent brick and slime. To become famous, they wanted to build a huge city and a tower with brick and slime. The prophetical Babylon is also known for her 'marvellous' inventions.

છ છ

CHAPTER XI

Why Not Rome?

L ocated on the river Tiber, Rome was founded by Romulus in 753 B.C. Over the years, it earned the sobriquets 'The City of Fountains,' 'The Eternal City' and 'The City of Seven Hills.'

Rome is an ancient country. It cannot be the prophetical Babylon on the following grounds:

(1) The Bible says "... the hindermost of the nations..." (Jer. 50: 12), implying that the prophetical Babylon should be a new country.

However, in 27 B.C. there arose a leader named Caesar Augustus, who became the first ruler of what came to be known as the Roman Empire. Known for its military strength, Rome ruled over Europe for 500 years. Though the Roman Empire collapsed 1,500 years ago, much of its technology is still the blueprint for modern living. Many new technologies, such as strengthened concrete and high-rise apartment blocks, are Roman inventions. Roman emperors used these technologies to build the Coliseum, the Pantheon and the Vespasian's amphitheatre. In its heyday, Rome was like the U.S.A of today—a superpower. But it gradually got reduced to being nothing more than the present-day Italy.

Jesus was not born in a free and independent Palestine. Palestine was under the Roman Empire. During those days, Caesar Augustus was the emperor and Herod the king of Palestine.

(2) She was the offspring of another nation. The Bible says, "Your mother shall be sore confounded; she that bare you shall be ashamed: "(Jer. 50:12). 'Mother' implies Babylon as the baby-child of another nation. It is nothing but an image. No one can undo God's promise. It was God's promise to Abraham that his descendants would be very wealthy, prosperous, powerful and become a great nation. These promises applied to Jacob as well. The almighty God appeared to Jacob to remind him of the blessings. "And God said unto him, I am God Almighty: be fruitful and multiply; a nation and a company of nations shall be of thee, and kings shall come out of thy loins" (Gen. 35:11). The third generation of Abraham, Joseph, the son of Jacob, was sold by his brothers down into Egypt, and he became a prosperous man. He was elevated to this status because it was his birthright. Even his descendants were destined to become as prosperous as Joseph himself (1 Chron. 5:2). The Almighty gave His blessings to Abraham through Joseph's sons, Ephraim and Manasseh.

In the sunset of his life, Jacob told Joseph: "And now the two sons, Ephraim and Manasseh, which were born unto thee in the land of Egypt before I came unto thee into Egypt, are mine; as Reuben and Simeon, they shall be mine." (Gen. 48:5). So, it is the eternal truth that stands.

That did happen when the king of Assyria conquered Israel (the northern kingdom) and took the Israelites into captivity to Assyria in 721 B.C. After the captive life in exile, when the exilic term was over, they were supposed to go back to Israel, but they did not. The ten tribes of Israel were lost. They had lost their identity. They became as good as the Gentiles, known by another name, speaking a different language.

On the other hand, Judah (the southern kingdom) was captured by Nebuchadrezzar, the king of Babylon, in 604 B.C. There was no other way out for the people of Judah but to go into captivity to Babylon. Jeremiah, the prophet, was among the captive Jews. A miracle took place and Jeremiah was free to go anywhere he liked. Soon after, he met the Israelites.

It was under the leadership of Jeremiah that the Israelites went to the northwest of Europe across the Mediterranean Sea. So the descendants of Ephraim and Manasseh came together with a "saint" (Jeremiah) to the most Northern Province of Ireland and landed in Ulster while some of them travelled to Scotland and finally came over to England.

What about the other eight tribes of Israel? Their descendants are to be found in the north-western and Northern Europe.

For quite a long time the descendants of Ephraim and Manasseh became the inhabitants of Great Britain. After a very long time, Columbus discovered American in 1492. Manasseh still remained with Ephraim till New England (America) was discovered. Originally, there were twelve tribes of Israel including Joseph. But when Joseph divided into two tribes (Ephraim and Manasseh) and Manasseh separated into an independent nation, it became the thirteenth tribe, for which, we see that in the beginning there were thirteen colonies in America.

The overwhelming modern fulfilment of prophecy, in proof of divine origin and inspiration, is the sudden sprouting of two nations, a 'nation' and a 'company of nations', from comparative obscurity to positions of world dominance, unprecedented wealth and power. The almighty God promised to bless their land, give them rain, and make them wealthy and prosperous. They were to become so powerful that they could defeat every enemy. God's promise was "...be fruitful and multiply: a nation and company of nations shall be of thee..." (Gen. 35:11).

In 1800 A.D., the United Kingdom and the United States were not considered as 'significant' nations. The United Kingdom consisted of only the British Isles, a very small part of India (Bengal, Bihar and Orissa), Canada and a few little islands. The United States consisted of only the original 13 colonies and 3 added states. Neither of them possessed any great wealth or power. On January 4th, 1776, 13 colonies became independent. On declaration of independence, there broke out a war between Great Britain and her 13 colonies in America. This war was America's War of Independence. After seven years, in 1783, the war ended and the 13 colonies got independence. Primarily, there were 13 states but afterwards another 7 states joined them. Later 30 territories joined them to make the number of states swell to 50.

However, beginning in 1800 A.D., these two little nations began to grow into vast powerful nations. After the First World War, the United States of America was regarded as one of the supreme powers, the other being the Soviet Union. After the disintegration of the Soviet Union in 1991, the United States of America became the most powerful nation on earth.

And "the sun never sets on the British Empire." Britain gave independence to her colonies, but all her colonies put together constitute the British Commonwealth of Nations. "The children which thou shall have (colonies) after thou hast lost the other (13 colonies, which became the United States of America) shall say again in thine ears, The place is too strait for me: give place to me that I may dwell" (Isaiah 49:

20). Great Britain was too small for the island dwellers; that is why, they went to the United States.

Together, the British grew into multitudes and then separated (the U.S.A). On the other side of the world, they discovered "New England," which is now the United States of America. The U.S.A separated from the Great Britain and became the greatest and wealthiest nation on earth.

Rome Does not have these Historical Characteristics

(3) Babylon in the Apocalypse does not denote Rome (Rev. 14: 8; 17:18; 18: 10, 16, 19) but does mean the "great city, (New York) which reigneth over the kings of the earth" (Rev. 17: 18). There are related verses that dislodge the correct location of the prophetical Babylon.

(4) So far as Rome is concerned, it is a city of seven hills, but John speaks about it figuratively. It is a prophetic symbol. For example, it is written in the Bible, "...I will tell thee the mystery of the woman, and of the beast that carrieth her, which hath seven heads and ten horns." The literal meaning of this would be, " I will tell you the mystery of the woman being carried by the beast having seven heads and ten horns." Its literal meaning amounts to a mockery. So far as the seven hills are concerned, if properly expounded, it may turn out to be another thing altogether. In this area, Bible scholars have always put square pegs in round holes. Taking it for a correct statement, the seven skyscrapers of Manhattan city could have been regarded as seven hills. The city of Manhattan is known for its skyscrapers. Bible scholars have been deceived by the idea of "seven hills." They are dead sure that it is Rome, but they are sadly mistaken, as it is New York City (particularly Manhattan).. Theologians and Bible scholars cling to the idea that Rome is the city of seven hills and that it is the prophetical Babylon. In the Bible, Babylon has been depicted, though deceptively, through figures and symbols.

(5) Manhattan is an island, as the Hudson River flows on her west, which is the main river. On her east is the East River, tidal strait. On her north is another tidal strait named Harlem River, which joins the Hudson River and the East River. And on her south, lies the Atlantic Ocean.

John saw in a vision that 'she' sits upon many waters. Jeremiah, the prophet, saw the sea is come upon Babylon and she is covered with the multitude of waves thereof. Jeremiah says, "O thou that dwellest upon many waters" (Jer. 51:13). Again, the Lord says through Jeremiah, "A drought is upon her water; and they shall be dried up... " (Jer. 50: 38). Through the same prophet the Lord says He would render Babylon "... a dry land and a desert" (Jer. 50:12).

Rome is not an island. The river Tiber flows from the north-east corner and gets into the Mediterranean Sea on her south-west corner. Though Rome faces the sea, it is not an island (many waters).

(6) The New York money market is the biggest money market in the world. The next big money market is the London money market. Jeremiah, the prophet, says, "abundant in treasurers" (Jer. 51:13). John refers to her as the 'queen'. America is the strongest nation of the world. Babylon is one of the most opulent cities of the world. It is not only the largest city, but also the financial capital of the U.S.A. This is why she gives financial aid to other nations. She lives like a queen.

It is said that the United States of America holds 52 percent of world's wealth. North-Western Europe has another big chunk of world's wealth. So, the richest nation, by far, is the United States of America.

When Christopher Columbus discovered America in 1492, America was an underdeveloped country. It started with 13 colonies, having neither wealth nor power. But the table turned in the 1800 A.D. Both the U.S.A and the Great Britain grew richer and ultimately the United States of America stood as an economic and political giant. Every American today is proud to live in New York—the richest city of America. But when we look back we find that New York was a Dutch colony in the mid-seventeenth century. It was like any other city in those days. But now she is regarded as the richest city in the whole world. Also, the main United Nations headquarters are located on the international territory in New York City.

On the contrary, the money market in Rome is not the richest money market in the world, nor does Rome rule over the "kings of the earth." Of course, a long time ago, she used to do just that. The Roman Empire was spread across the length and breadth of Europe, North Africa and Asia Minor. As far as the location of the Headquarters of the U.N. Organs and Agencies are concerned, there is only one in Rome—Food and Agriculture Organisation.

(7) She should be the 'hindermost of the nations' or the youngest of the nations. So far as Rome is concerned, it was built in 753 B.C. So, it is not a newly formed country. Even the Roman Empire, which began in 27 B.C., ended 1,500 years ago. America was discovered in 1492.

Therefore, it can be safely concluded that New York City and not Rome is the prophetical Babylon.

 C8 80

CHAPTER XII

A Glimpse of New York City

The characteristics of New York City exactly match the characteristics of the prophetical Babylon. The wonderful city of New York spreads over Manhattan and Staten Island, the western end of Long Island, a portion of the main land and various islands in New York harbour and Long Island Sounds. Its urban area extends into neighbouring parts of New York, New Jersey and Connecticut.

The city consists of five boroughs (Manhattan, Brooklyn, Queens, the Bronx and the Staten islands), which correspond to the five counties of New York State. All are located near the point where the Hudson River empties into the Upper New York Bay of the Atlantic Ocean. The city's only land boundaries are Westchester County in the north and the Nassau County on the Long Island in the east. The city's waterfront is used for shipping and recreation. New York City is the centre of the largest urban agglomeration in the United States. It is the largest city in the Western Hemisphere.

It is a cosmopolitan city. The Statue of Liberty has become more or less a symbol of refuge and opportunity.

New York City stands as the hub of global trade.' It is also famous for art, entertainment and fashion. As the city is the financial capital of the United States of America, it holds the headquarters of many of the world's largest corporations.

Wall Street in Manhattan is home to the nation's largest stock exchange and is the headquarters of the country's largest brokerage firms. New York City is the heart of the mass media in the United States. It holds the nation's television and radio network. It also holds the main offices of the largest advertising agencies. Most of the nation's publishing houses are based in midtown Manhattan.

Manhattan, a major commercial, financial and cultural centre of both the United States and the world, is the most densely populated of the five boroughs of New York City. It is known for its stupendous skyscrapers. Home to some of the nation's most valuable real estate, Manhattan is considered as one of the most expensive areas in the United States. It has a cosmopolitan character. New York City has large numbers of Italians, Puerto Ricans, Irish, Asians, West Indians and Jews.

Considering the character of the five boroughs, Staten Island is the most sub-urban. It is connected to Brooklyn by the Verrazeno-Narrows Bridge and to Manhattan via the Staten Island Ferry, which is one of the most popular tourist attractions in New York City. It provides a clear view of the Statue of Liberty, Ellis Island and Lower Manhattan. The Green Belt exists in Central Staten Island covering almost 25sq kilometres. The FDR Broadway along South Beach, the fourth largest in the world, is 20 miles long.

The Bronx is New York City's northernmost borough, the site of Yankee Stadium, home of New York Yankees and home to the largest co-operatively owned housing complex in the United States, co-operative city. Except for a small piece of Manhattan known as Marble Hill, the Bronx is the only section of the city that is part of the United States' mainland.

Like Manhattan, Brooklyn also has similar ethnic heterogeneity. It has commercial and industrial districts and residential areas. Brooklyn is the city's most populous borough and was an independent city until 1898. It is known for its cultural, social and ethnic diversity, independent art scene, distinct neighbourhood and a unique architectural heritage. It is also the only borough outside Manhattan with a distinct downtown area.

The second largest in population and the easternmost of the five boroughs of New York City, Queens is the largest in area. Queens is mainly residential and middle class people live there. It is the most ethnically diverse place in the United States. As far as the growth of population is concerned, it may overtake Brooklyn in the years to come. Originally a collection of small towns and villages founded by the Dutch, Queens has acquired the status of a borough of New York City.

CRROR

CHAPTER XIII

Map of Manhattan

Manhattan, a city of traffic, merchants of "many waters" (Rev. 17:1), pomp and show, skyscrapers (towers in the historical Babylon) and wealth will be consumed by fire.

If we study the map of Manhattan, we will find that it looks like an island. On the west side, the main River Hudson flows. On the east side, we come across the East River. On the north side, we see the River Harlem, connecting the Hudson River and the East River. On the south side is the majestic Atlantic Ocean.

There are a couple of tunnels under the Hudson River, one on the north and one on the south. The names are Lincoln Tunnel and Holland Tunnel, respectively. There is a tunnel called Queens Midtown Tunnel on the east side of Manhattan that runs under the East River, connecting Queens. Like the historical Babylon, there are tunnels under the River Hudson and the East River, respectively. Also, like the historical Babylon, the east side of the city is more significant of the two. This is a replica of the historical Babylon. On the east side of Hudson River stands Manhattan, high-headedly. It reminds us of Revelation 17:9; "the seven heads are seven mountains," i.e., the skyscrapers. How fitting is the answer! How amazing is the reply! Like the historical Babylon, Manhattan is a wonderful city.

So far as the bridges are concerned, over the East River in New York City, is the Queensboro Bridge, also known as the 59th Street Bridge. It connects the neighbourhood of Long Island City in the borough of Queens with Manhattan, passing over Roosevelt Island. The Williamsburg Bridge across the East River connects the Lower East Side of Manhattan with the Williamsburg neighbourhood of Brooklyn. The Manhattan Bridge connects Lower Manhattan with Brooklyn. And the Brooklyn Bridge connects the New York City boroughs of Manhattan and Brooklyn by spanning the East River.

I would like to take this opportunity to mention the heights of some of the skyscrapers in the United States:

- The World Trade Centre was 1,776 ft tall (each building). Both the buildings (as if two mountains) were destroyed in the 9/11 attacks. The attacks resulted in 2,752 deaths.

- The Empire State Building is 1,472 ft or 448 metres tall.

- The Chrysler Building is 1,046 ft or 319 metres tall.

- The Woolworth Building is 792 ft or 241 metres tall.

- The Flatiron Building is 285 ft or 87 metres tall.

The seven skyscrapers resemble the seven mountains (Rev. 17:9). The southern tip of the island, which is called the Financial District, is another vulnerable place, where the World Trade Centre was burned down. Another vulnerable place is the Upper East Side, where the United Nations Secretariat is located. In that case, the entire island of Manhattan will be a vulnerable place, followed by Brooklyn, Queens, the Bronx and Staten Island.

We must bear in mind that though New York would be the first place to be destroyed, ultimately, the entire world would be engulfed in the flames of annihilation.

The conclusion to which all these arguments lead is that New York, especially Manhattan, is the prophetical Babylon; it is a replica of the prophetical Babylon.

 CB EO

CHAPTER XIV
Eternal Silence

"And the voice of harpers, and musicians, and of pipers, and trumpeters, shall be heard no more at all in thee..." (Rev. 18:22).

"Because the Lord hath spoiled Babylon, and destroyed out of her the great voice; when her waves do roar like great waters, a noise of their voice is uttered" (Jer. 51:55).

The voice of harpers and musicians and of pipers and trumpeters shall be heard no more. Broadway, which represents the musicians, shall be silent forever. And Carnegie Hall, which is one of the most famous concert halls in the world, shall be silent forever. The silence shall be the silence of a vast graveyard.

ଔ ଓ

Scripture Index

 CB ED

Bibliography

The following books have been referred to in preparation of the text:

BOOKS

Bertrand Russell, *In Praise of Idleness*; Union Hymn Ltd. London, 1976

C.I. Scofield, *The First Scofield Reference Bible*, Believers Bookshelf Inc. Pennsylvania, U.S.A.

Dr. D.K. Das, Shalom Adam (Unpublished), 1996.

Etienne Charpentier, How to Read the Old Testament, Bombay,
    i. St. Pauls, 1993.

Good News New Testament, Today's English Version

Henry M. Morris – *The Remarkable Record of Job*, Master Books, California.

John Hargreaves, *A Guide Book of Genesis*, Delhi, ISPCK, 1993.

J.F. Horrabin, *Glimpses of World History*, New Delhi, Oxford Univ. Press, 1993.

John R. Rice, *Bible Lessons of the Book of Revelation*, Sword
Of the Lord Publishers, Tennessee, U.S.A.

Smith's Bible Dictionary, revised by Rev. F.N. and M.A. Peloubet, Zondarvan Pub. House, Michigan, 1976.

The Holy Bible: Containing the Old Testament and the New Testament,
King James Version, American Bible society, New York.

BOOKLET

Herbert W. Armstrong, *The British Commonwealth and the United States in Prophecy,* 1954.

 Cß ßð

www.ingramcontent.com/pod-product-compliance
Lightning Source LLC
LaVergne TN
LVHW011337080426
835513LV00006B/397